BECK & PAULI LITH. MILWAUKEE, WIS.

E CITY OF

RBOR,

GAN 1880

UNIVERSITIES OF MICHIGAN.

23. University Hall.
24. Department of Law.
25. Department of Medecine and Surgery
26. Hospital—Alopathic.
27. Homeopathic Medical College and Hospital.
28. Chemical Laboratory.
29. Dental College.
30. Museum of Science.
31. Museum of Art and History.
32. Boiler House.
33. Astronomical Observatory.
34. Presidents House.
35. Steam Carpenter's Shop.

36. Carriage & Sleigh Factory, C. Walker & Bros., Prop.
37. Carriage & Sleigh Fact'y, B. F. Arksey, Prop
38. "   "   "   A. R. Schmidt, "
39. Sash, Door & Blind Fact'y, Luick Bros., Prop.
40. "   "   "   H. Krapf, Prop.
41. Cabinet Fact'y, Rauschenberger & Co., Prop.
42. Triumph Wind Mill Factory, A. M. Bodwell Prop.
43. Soap and Potash Factory, A. Birk, Prop.
44. Tannery, J. Heinzman & Son, Prop.
45. "   Henry Krause, Prop.
46. Ferdon Lumber Yard, Jas. Tolbert, Prop.
47. Marble Yard, Anton Eisele Prop.
48. Cook House, C. H. & F. W. Jewell, Prop.
49. Hotel.
50. Agricultural Ware House, M. Rogers, Prop.
51. Green House, Cousins & Hall, Prop.
52. "   Jas. Toms, Prop.

THE UNIVERSITY OF MICHIGAN
A Pictorial History

The University of Michigan
A Sesquicentennial Publication

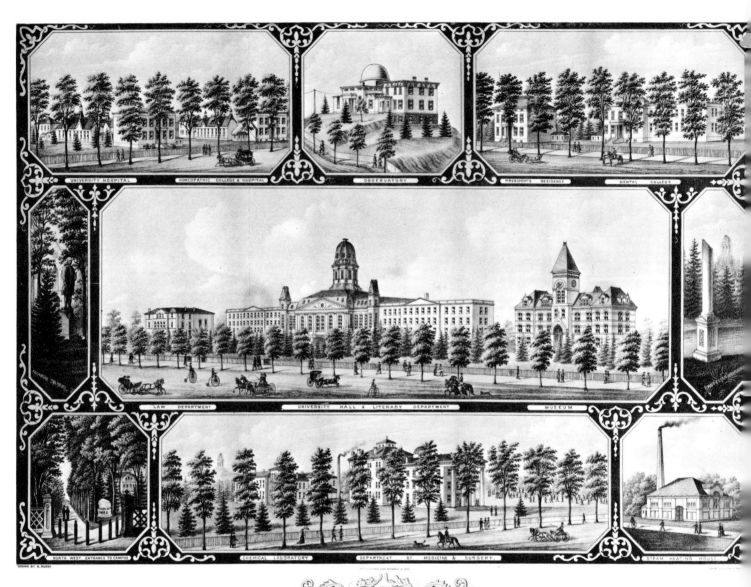

UNIVERSITY OF MICHIGAN

ANN ARBOR.

The University of Michigan

A PICTORIAL HISTORY

by
Ruth Bordin

Ann Arbor
THE UNIVERSITY OF MICHIGAN PRESS

Copyright © by The University of Michigan 1967
All rights reserved
Library of Congress Catalog Card No. 66-17029
Published in the United States of America by
The University of Michigan Press and simultaneously
in Rexdale, Canada, by Ambassador Books Limited
Manufactured in the United States of America

Book design by Quentin Fiore

Foreword

Compared with The University of Michigan, the Michigan Historical Collections are young. Founded thirty years ago with the blessing of President Alexander G. Ruthven and placed under the direction of Professor Lewis G. Vander Velde, they have become the depository of papers of numerous individuals and organizations throughout the state and also of University records. All these papers have been arranged, catalogued, and made available for research; most of the contents of this book have been drawn from these archival materials.

During the century and a half of its existence, The University of Michigan has developed from an institution with two professors and seven students into one of the foremost in the nation. It has always been noted for leadership in educational innovations, academic achievement, and intercollegiate athletics. The story of this remarkable career is graphically portrayed here. Beginning with the little-known Detroit period, this book provides a panoramic view of the whole fabric of the University through the administration of President Harlan Hatcher.

The treatment is both comprehensive and selective. Hundreds of photographs were examined in order to find those deemed most significant. There are pictures of student life and activities, organizations, publications, dramatic presentations, class rushes, social affairs, athletic contests, academic ceremonies, classrooms, buildings old and new, distinguished professors, and of the campuses which spread far beyond the boundaries of the original forty acres.

FOREWORD

Ruth Bordin was chosen to prepare this book because of her special competence. Having been for eight years curator of manuscripts and pictures in the Collections, she has a broad background of knowledge. Her creative imagination, insight, and lively style make both text and legends vivid supplements to the pictures. Dr. Robert M. Warner, assistant director of the Collections, collaborated with Mrs. Bordin in selecting the photographs.

The University's News Service, the colleges and departments, and Mr. Eck Stanger of the *Ann Arbor News* were generous in contributing photographs.

The Michigan Historical Collections present this book as part of their share in commemorating the sesquicentennial of The University of Michigan.

F. CLEVER BALD
Director

Contents

I

The University in Detroit

Be it enacted by the Governor and the Judges of the Territory of Michigan that there shall be in said Territory a Cathole-pistemiad ... or University, of Michigania.

So READ AN ACT passed on August 26, 1817, by the governor and judges who together formed the Territorial Legislature of Michigan, providing for Michigan's first educational system. Here was one of Michigan's bravest dreams—a remarkable piece of legislation, especially for an infant territory still struggling with the elemental problems of transportation, Indians, and settlement. In a community which boasted only a handful of learned men, thirteen didaxiim or professorships, embracing all facets of knowledge, were to be filled by men appointed by the governor. Not only were these professors to constitute a university faculty, but they were also to function as a Territorial Board of Education clothed with ample political power to supervise all schools and educational activities and to appoint all teachers, librarians, and curators. These didactors were to be paid from the public treasury. The governor and judges were empowered to raise the necessary funds by increasing existing taxes 15 percent. They were also given permission to hold four lotteries, proceeds of which would be used to procure suitable lands and buildings and establish libraries. The language of the Act was grandiose, almost ridiculous, but the concept was broad and remarkably prophetic. Most important, the principle of public support for a unified educational system was clearly spelled out.

In 1817 Detroit, the little territorial capital, was still recovering from the War of 1812. Farmers had been systematically plundered by the Indians, the fur trade virtually suspended, and the citizens forced to submit to British occupation for over a year. Its population was not much more than 1500. The entire territory contained about 7,000 people, and only the lands in the southeastern corner of the present state had as yet been ceded by the Indians and opened to settlement. Although a few American civilians had found their way to the little community, Detroit's population was still largely French-Canadian with a sprinkling of British left over from their period of control, and the mainstay of the economy continued to be the fur trade.

To plan for education on such a scale as outlined in the Act of 1817 was certainly bold, but the infant territory was not without bold spirits. The prime mover behind the ambitious scheme which envisaged for this raw western land a system of colleges, academies, libraries, museums, botanic gardens, laboratories, and the like, was Augustus Brevoort Woodward, whom Thomas Jefferson had appointed judge of the Supreme Court of Michigan Territory in 1805. Native of New York state, graduate of Columbia College, Washington lawyer, real-estate speculator, and friend of Thomas Jefferson, Woodward was an unpredictable, misunderstood, and uncouth bachelor. He was also a man of imagination and drive, concerned with all facets of the territory's activities. His creative ideas on a host of subjects from city planning to high finance kept the little community supplied with its share of controversy. His educational ideas stemmed from two sources. He had been influenced in his view of the organization of knowledge by John Locke's *Essay on Human Understanding*, and he was also aware of Napoleon's schemes for a centralized French educational system. More important, he had shared with Thomas Jefferson plans for implementing these ideas through a formal educational institution rooted in some part of America.

It is not surprising that Woodward's restless and eccentric intellect brought forth this plan, or that he consulted widely with over a score of prominent men including Jefferson, James Madison, and John Randolph in its formulation. What is more startling is that parts of his ambitious dream were actually implemented. Within a month of the Act's passage Acting Governor William Woodbridge had appointed as president of the Catholepistemiad the Reverend John Monteith, a twenty-nine-year-old graduate of the College of New Jersey (now Princeton) and an ordained Presbyterian clergyman who ministered to Detroit's interdenominational First Protestant Society. For vice-president he chose Father Gabriel Richard, a French priest who had lived in Detroit for nineteen years and who from the beginning of his Detroit pastorate had acted as schoolmaster to the little community. Richard had long urged a more comprehensive educational system than he could provide by his own efforts. Richard and Monteith were among the best educated men in the territory. Between them they filled the thirteen professorships of the Catholepistemiad, and as educational officers of the territory they proceeded to implement the Act further.

An official seal was adopted for the institution on September 12, 1817, and that same month the cornerstone of the first building was laid on the west side of Bates Street near Congress Street, subscriptions amounting to over $5000 having been obtained to finance the work. Funds remaining from the contributions for the relief of the sufferers in the Detroit fire of 1805 were also allocated to the new body. Although the special taxes and lotteries authorized by the Act of 1817 were never levied or drawn, the principle of public support was honored, at least in part, for the judges voted $500 toward the building and $80 toward purchase of the lot. A year later the building was actually in use to house an English school on the Lancastrian model. By 1819 an orthodox classical academy was in operation, under the supervision of the didactors, which featured Latin, Greek, French, and English "grammatically taught," together with writing, composition, rhetoric, geography, arithmetic, surveying, bookkeeping, and navigation. Neither of these schools was free, but the tuition charged was only one to three dollars a quarter. At one time 183 students were enrolled in the Lancastrian school, and educational activities continued in the Bates Street building under University auspices until 1833.

In name and language the Catholepistemiad reeked of pompous pedantry. Its pretentious plan for a comprehensive educational system was far beyond the scope of the territory's scant resources. Judge Woodward truly was ahead of his time, but the principles on which his grandiose scheme for education was based were sound.

First, he made the territory responsible for educating its people from primary classes through the university. In 1817, when even elementary education was considered the responsibility of parents, this was an advanced idea indeed. Second, he envisaged a system supported by taxation, although it would be many years before taxpayers would accept the cost of educating other persons' children. Third, tuition charges in the University were to be moderate, and the government should pay for the higher education of those whose parents could not afford it. Last, the schools and the University should be secular. This principle, at a time when all colleges were maintained by religious denominations, was also radical, but eventually all of these principles were accepted in Michigan and elsewhere.

In 1821 the Reverend John Monteith left Detroit to take a professorship of ancient languages at Hamilton College, Clinton, New York. Prior to his departure, the governor and judges on April 30 replaced the Act of 1817 with a new law establishing the University of Michigan in Detroit. Judge Woodward did not sign this act. Perhaps he resented the use of simple English in a document of such serious import. Instead of government by president and faculty as provided in the law of 1817, a board of twenty-one trustees was named to manage the institution. The governor was ex-officio a member and chairman of the board. Others named in the act were leading citizens of the town, including Monteith and Richard. These trustees were the corporate organization of the University, inheriting the didactors' functions. They were capable of suing and being sued, of holding, buying, and selling property, and of adopting a common seal, and they had power to establish colleges, academies, and schools in the territory. Actually, their chief contribution was the management of university property. Besides the building in Detroit and three sections given by the Indians at the urging of Governor Lewis Cass in the treaty of 1817, two townships had been granted for the support of a "seminary of learning" by Congress in 1826.

Although for more than a century the Regents of The University of Michigan ignored the significance of the Catholepistemiad, in 1929 they finally recognized its contribution by authorizing 1817 as the date on the official seal. Their action was sound, for in 1856 the Supreme Court of Michigan had decided that the Regents of The University of Michigan in Ann Arbor were the lawful successors of the Trustees of the Catholepistemiad, and the University as we know it has benefitted from the lands originally granted to the Catholepistemiad.

Father Gabriel Richard. This portrait was painted at Montreal for M. Antoine Jeaubien.

Judge Augustus B. Woodward may have resembled this sketch when he was judge of Michigan Territory. No portrait of him exists, and this drawing was made from verbal description.

Photo: Joseph Klima, Jr.

Detroit was a sparsely settled village in 1820 when sketched from the Canadian shore by George Washington Whistler, father of James McNeil Whistler. The "Walk-in-the-Water," in the foreground, brought many early settlers to Detroit.

The books which Monteith owned when he was president of the Cathole-pistemiad are now in the Michigan Historical Collections.

Monteith's papers, quill pen, and a volume of Thomas à Kempis given him by Father Richard.

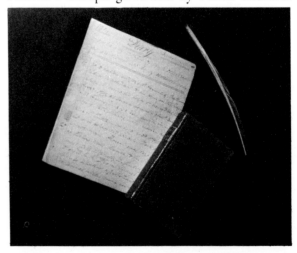

The first seal of the University
of Michigan was adopted by
President Monteith and Vice-
President Richard, in September
1817. It was probably never
used, since documents signed
by Monteith bear only a plain
wafer.

John Monteith wrote this letter September 18, 1817, to William Woodbridge, secretary of the Territory, accepting appointment to several professorships in the University of Michigania.

[7]

A table of the Professorships of a University, constructed on the principles of the epistemic system.

I. The nearest familiar and elegant names adapted to the English language.	II. The epistemic names which may be engrafted, without variation, into every modern language.	III. The number of the particular sciences comprehended in the several professorships.
I. Literature	I. Anthroposglossica	8.
II. Mathematics	II. Mathematica	5.
III. Natural History	III. Physiognostica	4.
IV. Natural Philosophy	IV. Physicosophica	6.
V. Astronomy	V. Astronomia	1.
VI. Chemistry	VI. Chymia	1.
VII. The Medical Sciences	VII. Iatrica	8.
VIII. The Œconomical Sciences	VIII. Œconomica	5.
IX. The Ethical Sciences	IX. Ethica	4.
X. The Military Sciences	X. Polemitactica	8.
XI. The Historical Sciences	XI. Diegetica	6.
XII. The Intellectual Sciences	XII. Ennœica	7.
XIII. Universal Science	XIII. Catholepistemia	63.

The table of professorships of the University of Michigania is in Augustus Woodward's own handwriting.

This building on Bates Street near Congress Street was built by the officers of the Catholepistemiad and used for several years as a school under University auspices, the site of the first state-sponsored education in Michigan.

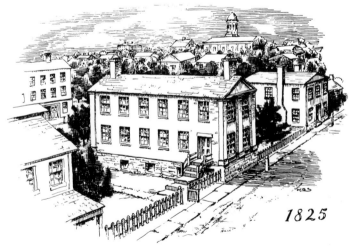

1825

II

The Ann Arbor Beginnings (1837-71)

IN 1835 ISAAC CRARY, a young lawyer living in the little settlement of Marshall, Michigan, read Victor Cousin's report to the French minister of public instruction on *The State of Education in Prussia*. Crary was impressed with the centralized state-supported system Cousin described, and as a member of Michigan's first Constitutional Convention in 1835 and chairman of its education committee, he was in a position to implement the ideas Cousin's report suggested.

Michigan's first constitution, which Crary helped to write, required the legislature to establish common schools and a university and provided for a superintendent of Public Instruction, a constitutional officer who was to head a unified educational system on a modified Prussian model which could even exercise some control over local common schools. The constitution also prohibited state monies being used for sectarian institutions, a common practice in other states, which meant that in Michigan all state resources for higher education would go to strengthen the University.

In 1835 young Crary and his bride were living with John D. Pierce, a clergyman who had come to Marshall the previous year under the auspices of the Presbyterian Home Missionary Society. Pierce and Crary had spent many hours discussing Cousin's report and the kind of educational system Michigan should aspire to, and Crary recommended that Governor Stevens T. Mason appoint Pierce as the first superintendent of Public Instruction. Pierce informed himself further by studying Eastern school systems and

[9]

drew up a comprehensive report which served as the basis for Michigan's first school legislation, passed in 1837 two months after statehood was achieved. These acts provided for a university with literary, law, and medical departments, branches of that university to serve as the state's secondary school system, and local common schools. By 1837 the population of Michigan was nearly 100,000, in contrast to 7000 in 1817 when the Catholepistemiad was conceived. This time a comprehensive plan had an excellent chance to succeed.

Citizens of Ann Arbor, eager to profit from the projected institution of higher learning, won out over other communities competing for the University. The newly appointed University Regents were offered the forty-acre site which still forms the central campus square, and plans to erect the University's first buildings were made. In 1837 Ann Arbor was only fourteen years old, but it had a population of two thousand, and the village boasted a courthouse, a jail, a bank, four churches, three mills, eleven lawyers, and nine physicians, as well as a flourishing academy with seventy pupils. The Regents at first hoped to add a touch of authentic grandeur to the institution and hired a well-known New Haven architect to draw an elaborate plan for the campus that would have cost a half million dollars. But lagging sales of University lands and veto of the proposal by the more realistic superintendent of Public Instruction forced the substitution of a modest plan. Six buildings in all were to be erected—two dormitory-classroom buildings along the State Street side of the square, only one of which was to be built immediately, and four houses for professors, two on North University and two on South University, all facing toward the center of the campus.

Four years were required to construct the buildings and ready them for use. Instruction began in the five preparatory-school Branches of the University in 1838, with 161 students on hand, but not until the fall of 1841 were the two professors, George Palmer Williams and Joseph Whiting, and seven students assembled at Ann Arbor for the actual beginning of formal instruction in the University. There were more Regents (eighteen) than faculty and students combined that first year. Admission fees were only ten dollars plus an additional $2.50 collected each term. Expenditures for University purposes averaged $8252 a year for the first years. Since it was soon obvious that the sale of University lands would not provide enough money for both the University and the Branches, support for the Branches was withdrawn, and they ceased to be part of the University. By the academic year 1851-52 the faculty of the growing University had increased to six, and sixty-two students were in attendance.

The University had no president in these early years—a chancellorship rotated among the professors—but the new state constitution of 1850, which gave the University constitutional status and greater independence, required the Regents to appoint a president. On the recommendation of the historian George Bancroft, they chose a man of great talent and ability, Henry Philip Tappan, a New Yorker and graduate of Union College. He was a well-known philosopher whose books received recognition in Europe as well as in the United States. He had just returned from a lengthy tour of European universities, much impressed, like Cousin, by what he saw in Germany. He was eager to create "an American University deserving of the name," which would be a part of a public-school system. He saw no hope of achieving this goal in the conservative East, but believed the state of Michigan offered him his opportunity.

Tappan guided the little college at Ann Arbor toward a true university status. Under his auspices graduate studies were begun, scientific courses were added to the Literary Department, and Michigan became the second university in the country to grant a bachelor of science degree. Although the Medical Department had been opened in 1850, the Law Department, also provided for in the Act of 1837, was added during Tappan's incumbency. Space to provide for this rapidly growing institution, whose enrollment tripled during the Tappan years, was obtained by eliminating dormitory quarters in the college buildings and converting them to classroom use.

Perhaps the most important of Tappan's accomplishments was reinforcing and replacing some of the early faculty of clergymen with young, well-trained men of intellectual distinction. Francis Brünnow, assistant to the director of the Royal Observatory in Berlin, came to Ann Arbor to head the new Observatory. Andrew Dickson White arrived fresh from studies in European universities to fill the first permanent chair of history in the country. Alexander Winchell, Corydon L. Ford, Henry Simmons Frieze, and James O. Boise were among Tappan's other appointments.

Tappan's last years at the University were not happy ones. His imperious manner alienated many of the townspeople, some of his faculty, and most of the Regents, especially after 1858 when a completely new board was elected. The new Regents, only four of whom had attended college, were determined to rule. Numerous clashes resulted and on June 25, 1863, the Regents met after Commencement exercises and summarily dismissed the president. Dr. Tappan deeply resented their cavalier action. He left Ann Arbor and made his home in Europe, never to return. Students, alumni, and many others protested bitterly. Letters were written and demonstrations were held, but these efforts were of no avail.

As successor, the Regents appointed Dr. Erastus O. Haven, who had been professor of Latin and English literature in the University from 1852 until 1856. He was mild and conciliatory and during his previous residence had made many friends. Although at first he was embarrassed by attempts of Tappan's supporters to have Tappan reinstated, Haven's calm, diplomatic conduct soon had the University on an even keel. His principal achievement was in inducing the legislature to provide regular financial support for the University over and above the monies obtained from the University lands. During his presidency the legislature stipulated that the income from one-twentieth of a mill on every dollar of property taxed by the state should be turned over to the University Regents. In 1869 this amounted to only $15,000. However, the legislature had accepted the principle that the state had a responsibility to support the University, and as the tax base increased so did the annual appropriation. The millage rate itself, raised several times in later years, provided the basis for University support until the state property tax was repealed in 1935.

As early as 1850 individuals and groups urged that women be admitted to the University, but Regents and faculty were reluctant to take so revolutionary a step. In 1867 the legislature recommended the admission of women, and President Haven favored the proposal shortly before he resigned. Although many of the faculty and most of the male students were still unconvinced, the Regents in January 1870 resolved that every resident of Michigan who possessed "the requisite literary and moral qualifications" had a right to enter the University. Miss Madelon Stockwell of Kalamazoo promptly presented herself as an applicant and after passing entrance examinations was enrolled as a sophomore. Other young ladies entered the next fall, and in the spring of 1871 one woman received a degree in law, another, a degree in medicine, and two, degrees in pharmaceutical chemistry. Five years after Miss Stockwell's enrollment one hundred women were studying at the University.

In 1869 Dr. Haven resigned to become president of Northwestern University, and Henry Simmons Frieze, professor of Latin, was appointed acting president. His interim administration's great contribution to the development of the University was the acceptance of high-school graduates without examination from schools which had been inspected and approved by a University faculty committee. This insured that the University would set standards for the secondary schools of the state and once more fulfill its original function as head of a unified system of education.

Isaac Crary, graduate of Trinity College, came to Michigan from Connecticut in 1833. Not only did he participate in the first constitutional convention, he also served as territorial delegate to Congress and was Michigan's first United States representative. He was appointed a regent of the University, by Governor Stevens T. Mason in 1837 and served until 1844.

The Ann Arbor Land Company gave forty acres to the University of Michigan for a campus. Its promoters hoped to make money selling the adjacent property advertised in the poster.

Splendid Sale of Real Estate
IN ANN ARBOR,
AT AUCTION!!

THE undersigned will offer at Public Auction on the 8th day of June next, at the Ann Arbor Exchange, in this Village, on the most liberal terms,

1000 VILLAGE LOTS,

comprising some of the most eligible locations for business, and many of the most delightful sites for dwellings in the village or its vicinity. Also,

100 Out Lots

of from 1 to 10 acres each, lying within one mile of the Village; several of them well timbered and many of them well watered, affording excellent pasture. Also a number of

IMPROVED FARMS

situated from one to three miles from town.

The healthy and delightful situation of Ann Arbor and its superior natural advantages are too well known to require description. The Legislature at its last session established the University at Ann Arbor; and also provided by law for the speedy construction by the State of the Detroit and St. Joseph Rail Road, which will probably be completed to this place the present season. The funds of the University being now estimated at over $5,000,000 and rapidly increasing, every thing connected with the institution will doubtless be conducted upon a scale of unparalleled munificence, and nothing will be omitted which science, taste, and wealth can do to embellish the Town, improve the society, and make it the most desirable residence in the Great West, for persons of Literature and refinement, while the great Agricultural, Manufacturing, and Commercial advantages of the place, and the facilities of communication with every part of the Union will afford ample employment for the capitalist and man of business. Similar inducements can never again be offered to purchasers in Michigan.

The terms of sale will be one fourth down, (or approved Bank paper,) and the balance in three equal annual instalments with annual interest secured upon the property. Ann Arbor Scrip will be received at $200 per share, in payment for all property sold by the Ann Arbor Land Co. ☞The sales will be positive, and the title in all cases warranted good.

E. W. MORGAN,   } Trustees of the Ann
WM. S. MAYNARD, } Arbor Land Co,
CHARLES THAYER,   D. B. BROWN,
CHESTER INGALLS,   E. S. COBB,
WM. R. THOMPSON,

Ann Arbor, April 20th, 1837.

One of the affiliated secondary schools which made up the University's branches in the 1840's occupied this building in Kalamazoo.

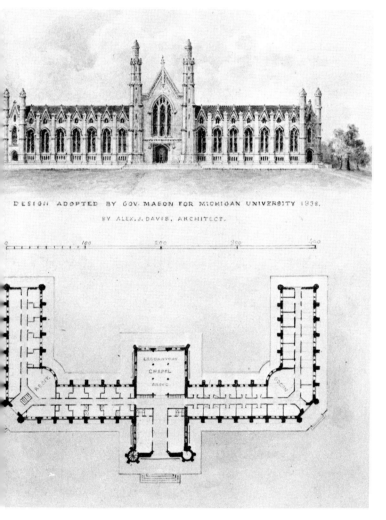

DESIGN ADOPTED BY GOV. MASON FOR MICHIGAN UNIVERSITY 1938.
BY ALEX.J.DAVIS, ARCHITECT.

Drawings for a University building made by Alexander J. Davis, New Haven architect. The building would have cost half a million dollars, and the plan was vetoed by John D. Pierce.

Photo: The Metropolitan Museum of Art, Dick Fund, 1924

The University Building, as it was originally known, was completed in 1841 at a cost of $16,000. Four stories high and of stucco over brick construction, it housed classrooms and student living quarters. The building was named Mason Hall in 1843 after Michigan's first governor, Stevens T. Mason. South Wing, known as South College, was completed in 1848. Also designed for classrooms and as a dormitory, it later housed the Law Department (until 1863) and non-laboratory engineering (until 1890).

The campus during Tappan's administration, from a small painting of 1855 by Jasper F. Cropsey, popular American landscapist. The scene was still pastoral. As late as 1846 the campus had been covered in summer with golden wheat grown by a janitor as part of his remuneration, and faculty families still harvested peaches from the orchard of the old Rumsey farm.

From an etching, made after a painting of the University buildings by J. F. Cropsey.

Henry Philip Tappan, the University's first president, was an eloquent speaker who fired the students' enthusiasm. He was forceful in his leadership, but overbearing and tactless.

Right: George Palmer Williams, University of Vermont graduate, attended Andover Theological Seminary and was an ordained Episcopal minister. In 1837 he was called to the University Branch at Pontiac. When the University opened in Ann Arbor he became professor of natural philosophy, later occupying the chairs of mathematics and physics.

Bottom, Left: Corydon La Ford was called from the University of Vermont to the professorship of anatomy in the University Medical Department in 1854. The association was to last for forty years. His reputation as a lecturer helped to draw several generations of medical students to Ann Arbor.

Bottom, Right: Franz Friedrich Ernst Brünnow, with a doctorate from the University of Berlin, had already published his work on spherical astronomy when Tappan brought him to Ann Arbor as the Observatory's first director in 1853. He married Tappan's daughter. When the president was dismissed in 1863, Brünnow resigned and returned to Europe, becoming professor of astronomy at the University of Dublin and Astronomer Royal for Ireland.

The Detroit Observatory as depicted by J. F. Cropsey. Completed in 1854, this gift of generous Detroiters, led by Henry N. Walker, who responded to Tappan's plea for contributions to the University, was situated on four acres of high land outside the city limits and overlooking the Huron River. It was furnished with excellent instruments, among them an astronomical clock and meridian circle, purchased by Tappan on his trip to Germany in 1853. From the beginning the Observatory was a leading astronomical installation in the United States.

The Chemical Laboratory, erected in 1856, now part of the Economics Building, was one of the first buildings in the world devoted exclusively to laboratory instruction in chemistry. Originally a one-story structure, various additions were made over the years. It was the University's principal Chemical Laboratory until 1909.

[20]

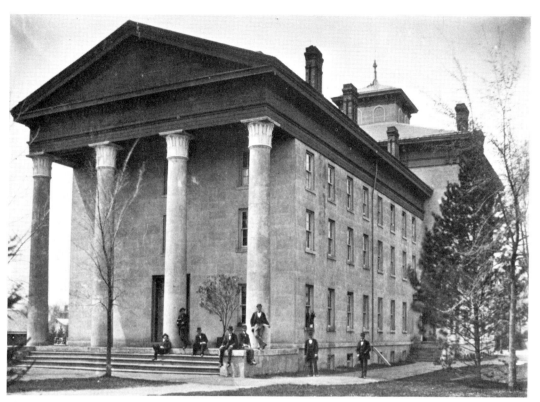

The first Medical Building was authorized in 1847 when $5000 was first set aside for the purpose. Another $3000 was forthcoming in 1848, and by 1850 the building was ready for occupancy. Professor Silas H. Douglas, a member of the first medical faculty, supervised its construction. Greek Revival in style and three stories high, it contained laboratories and lecture rooms, including a large amphitheater on the third floor lighted by a small dome. An addition was constructed in 1864, paid for in part by a general tax on the citizens of Ann Arbor. The enlarged building served as the center of medical education on the campus for more than fifty years.

Janitor Nagele, sometimes called "Doc" by the students, rang his bell in the Medical Building during the Tappan era.

Thomas McIntyre Cooley was admitted to the bar in Adrian, Michigan, in 1846. One of the state's distinguished young lawyers, he became one of the original faculty when the University's Law School opened in 1859. He filled the Jay professorship of law with distinction for the next quarter century. During his tenure he also served as a justice of the Michigan Supreme Court, where his opinions gained him national fame. In 1887 President Cleveland appointed him to the first Interstate Commerce Commission.

James Robinson Boise, a graduate and faculty member of Brown University until 1852, came to Michigan as professor of Greek language and literature with Tappan. His excellent scholarship added prestige to the classical curriculum for sixteen years.

James Valentine Campbell was one of the Law School's original faculty. He taught until 1885. He also practiced law in Detroit and served as a member of the state Supreme Court.

[22]

Alexander Winchell held chairs in physics, civil engineering, geology, paleontology, zoology, and botany at one time or another during his University career. He left Michigan briefly for the University of Syracuse in the 1870's, but returned in 1879. His major scientific contributions include descriptions of 308 new species of fossils. A devout Methodist, Winchell was able to reconcile his religious beliefs with Darwin's revolutionary theories when they made their initial impact on the scientific community.

Andrew Dickson White's first teaching post was at the University, where he occupied the first permanent chair of history in the country. Later, he was president of Cornell and ambassador to Germany.

"Nydia," a work in marble of Randolph Rogers, a popular midcentury American sculptor and resident of Ann Arbor as a young man, was presented to the University in 1860 by the Ann Arbor Art Association. Ann Arbor and its citizens made many gifts to the University.

Erastus Otis Haven, who returned to the University as its president in 1863, possessed the personal qualities necessary to heal the wounds caused by Tappan's dismissal. A Methodist clergyman and Wesleyan graduate, he had served as an academy principal in the East before coming to Michigan for the first time in 1852 as professor of Latin, a position he held until 1856.

[24]

The Ann Arbor Beginnings (1837-71)

The University faculty during Haven's administration assembled on
the steps of Mason Hall. Professors Douglas, Williams, Frieze,
Haven, Sager, and Palmer stand in the front row.

The early campus was bare and unkempt, and with little shade. A double row of trees was
planted around it in 1854, the outer row being provided by the citizens of Ann Arbor and the
inner by the professors and students. Most of these trees died, but in 1858 a more
successful attempt at planting was made. The Law Building, later known as
Haven Hall, is in the foreground of this view of 1865.

[25]

Moses Coit Tyler was brought to the chair of rhetoric and English literature in 1867, during the Haven administration.

Over a thousand alumni, former students, and staff members of the University served in the Civil War. Charles Kendall Adams (left) headed a voluntary company which trained on campus. He became professor of history at the University and later was president of the University of Wisconsin.

Henry Simmons Frieze, although he served in 1869-71 as president of the University and twice later as acting president, made his chief contribution during his long tenure at Ann Arbor as beloved teacher and musician. Boston-born and educated at Brown, he studied at the University of Berlin after his Michigan appointment, greatly broadening and deepening both his scholarship and his conception of higher education. Among his many lasting services to the University was his active role in founding the University Musical Society.

[27]

III

The Angell Years
(1871-1909)

COMMENTING IN HIS *Reminiscences* over forty years later, President James Burrill Angell wrote that when he arrived on Michigan's campus in 1871, he found an institution that "was shaped under broader and more generous views of university life than most of the eastern colleges." Angell was paying his intellectual debts to Crary, Pierce, and Tappan when he wrote these words. But they also illustrate that ambitious and thoughtful men still saw the only major university west of the Alleghenies as a fruitful field for testing new ideas and widening the scope of university life.

Angell had not made his decision to come to Ann Arbor without soul-searching, and many of his friends were consulted as to its wisdom. Those with Western experience, such as Andrew D. White, Henry Frieze (who had first suggested Angell's name), and Heman Wayland (then at Kalamazoo College), enthusiastically urged his acceptance. Others who were completely Eastern in outlook raised many questions as to the wisdom of such a choice. Actually, it was two years from the first call in 1869 until Angell assumed the position that was to occupy him with such profit to himself and the institution he served for the rest of his life.

Angell was forty-two when he began the longest tenure of any president in the history of the University of Michigan. Descended from stock that had migrated to Rhode Island with Roger Williams, he had been both student and professor at Brown University and later editor of the *Providence Journal* before accepting the presidency of the University of Vermont in 1866.

He described his first week in Ann Arbor as one of "fearful solicitude." Certainly, he faced his share of problems during the early years. The faculty and students were still opposed to coeducation, the student body was prone to rowdy pranks and undisciplined behavior—which gentle, kindly Frieze had never been able to control—and the controversy over the wisdom of founding a homeopathic medical school and deciding whether it should be located at Ann Arbor was at its height. None of Angell's predecessors had lasted very long. The West might be quick to provide opportunities for creative innovators, but it had not been loathe on occasion to remove them almost as rapidly.

In 1871 the University of Michigan had three flourishing colleges—Literature, Medicine, and Law. Nine buildings, including the four professors' houses, graced the campus and a faculty of thirty-five instructed a student body of more than twelve hundred. Although over half of its student body was in the Medical and Law schools, Michigan was the largest university in the United States, and its annual expenditures topped $100,000. Nonetheless, it was Angell's leadership which insured that the University would surmount the problems it faced in 1871 and not decline into a second-rate institution. Like Tappan, Pierce, and Crary before him, Angell was fully convinced of the importance of the University as an essential part of the state's educational system. He also believed that state and University would prosper or decline together. If Michigan moved forward so would the University, and the University's gains would in turn be translated into gains for the state.

Angell continued and strengthened many policies initiated by his predecessors. He lent all the weight of his office to overcoming the opposition to coeducation and making it work, for he sincerely believed that the University-educated woman had much to contribute in the staffing of the state's normal and high schools. He supported without reservation the supervision of high-school standards by the University and served for twenty-five years as chairman of the committee which visited the state's secondary schools to determine whether they met the criteria for admission of their students by diploma only. Later, as the Michigan system spread, he served as first president of the North Central Association of Colleges and Secondary Schools. He obtained increased tax support for the University and eventually obtained three-eighths of a mill of the state property tax for University purposes.

The Angell administration was also marked by many innovations. The curriculum of the Literary College was made much more flexible, and Latin and Greek were removed from the requirements for a bachelor of arts degree. In the 1870's Charles Kendall Adams introduced the seminar method of graduate instruction, and laboratories and clinical teaching in the sciences and medicine were extended and improved. Requirements for admission to the professional schools, largely nonexistent in the early years, were made increasingly rigorous. A formal budget as a method of controlling and planning the use of University financial resources was introduced in 1894, replacing the previous haphazard authorization of expenditures after they occurred. Foreign students, especially from China after Angell's ministry there, began to appear on campus in increasing numbers.

During the Angell administration the University rapidly began to resemble in size and organization the institution we know today. New schools, colleges, and departments were founded in quick succession. In 1875 the College of Dental Surgery and a Homeopathic Medical School opened their doors, followed in 1876 by a separate Department of Pharmacy. In 1879 William H. Payne was called to the first professorship in the science and art of teaching in the United States and from his work and that of his successor, Burke Hinsdale, the College of Education evolved. In 1881 a short-lived School of Political Science was organized, interesting because in many ways it foreshadowed the interdisciplinary centers of the mid-twentieth century. Graduate studies became a separate department in 1892, and the first beginnings of a summer school date from 1894. Engineering severed its earlier ties with the Literary College and emerged as a separate school in 1895, and a Department of Forestry under Filibert Roth was formally organized in 1903, growing out of courses given the previous year in the Botany Department.

Fifty buildings were constructed during Angell's long tenure, of which several remain today, among them Tappan Hall, Waterman Gymnasium, and the West Medical and West Engineering buildings. The number of faculty members greatly increased, and many distinguished scholars and scientists found their way to Ann Arbor. Among those who came for awhile but left again to make their major contributions elsewhere were John Jacob Abel, William LeBarron Jenney, and John Dewey. Mortimer E. Cooley in engineering, Victor Vaughan and Frederick G. Novy in medicine, Henry M. Bates in law, Henry Carter Adams in economics, Charles Horton Cooley in sociology, and Moses Gomberg in chemistry were among the many distinguished men who stayed. Dozens of others could be added to this list, for by the beginning of the new century the faculty was among the most distinguished bodies of scholars in the United States.

Along with the innovations and the foreshadowing of what was to come, the period of Angell's administration retained much of the flavor of the little provincial college. For many years President Angell served both as registrar of the University and dean of the Literary College, and until his first prolonged absence from the campus in 1880-81, when he served as United States minister and envoy plenipotentiary to China, he prided himself on knowing every student, at least in the Literary College, by name. Until 1895 he conducted morning chapel services for the students, and he usually preached the baccalaureate sermon on the Sunday evening preceding commencement, expounding a practical Christianity designed to aid the students in shaping a workable, ethical system by which they might live. He also taught international law until his retirement.

The only seriously disruptive incident to mark his presidency came toward the end of his first decade in Ann Arbor. The celebrated Rose-Douglas controversy ostensibly involved Assistant Professor Preston Rose's inability to account for a shortage in the fees which he personally collected from chemistry students. Actually, rivalry between the Methodists and other Protestant denominations and regental factionalism were the chief contributors to the bitter controversy which engaged state, University, and town for two years. Wounds were so deep that few of Angell's friends expected him to remain in Ann Arbor. Andrew D. White offered him succor at Cornell, and Michigan Congressman Jonas H. McGowan cautioned him not to close his "eyes or ears to offers to go elsewhere." But Angell had faith in the University and enough perspective to know that the losses, great as they were to the University's prestige and financial condition, could eventually be overcome.

In January 1905 Angell celebrated his seventy-sixth birthday. A few days later he submitted his resignation to the Board of Regents. Except for absences during his diplomatic missions to China and Turkey and with the International Fisheries Commission he had served the University continually nearly thirty-five years, and he sincerely felt that the time had come for his replacement by a younger man. Many others shared his feeling that more vigorous leadership was necessary, but the Regents believed otherwise and Angell's resignation was not accepted. Four years later the retirement of an eighty-year-old president could be postponed no longer. Angell's resignation was regretfully accepted by the Regents, who paid him tribute in these words: "The proud position which this University has attained is due, more than to all other elements combined, to the fact that for more than one-half its entire life it has been blessed with his learning, his culture, his wisdom, his tact and, above all, with the example and inspiration of his high-minded, Christian character."

President Angell had this photograph taken in Detroit in 1875, four years after he first came to Ann Arbor. He grew a beard to protect his sensitive throat against the persistent infections that plagued him as a young man and forced him to abandon the ministry as a career.

Ann Arbor's Main Street was complete with hitching posts and mud when Angell arrived in Ann Arbor.

Barns, orchard, and vegetable garden graced the rear of the President's House during the Angell administration. Angell demanded the installation of an indoor toilet as a condition of accepting the Michigan offer, and the third story was also added at his request.

Angell with members of the faculty shortly after he came to Ann Arbor. Left to right, front row, M. L. D'Ooge, C. K. Adams, H. S. Frieze, Angell, B. F. Cocker, E. Olney; second row, J. W. Langley, C. E. Greene, A. B. Prescott, A. Hennequin, C. S. Denison, O. C. Johnson, V. M. Spalding, W. H. Pettee; rear, P. R. DePont, J. B. Steere, I. N. Demmon, —, C. N. Jones.

The first University Hospital was attached to the original professor's house situated where the Natural Science Building now stands. The house alone was first used as a receiving home for patients, but in 1876 the attached pavilions were completed at a cost of $12,000. Additions were made in 1879 and 1881, and this enlarged Hospital remained the center of clinical instruction until 1891. The medical students were usually older than the literary students.

[35]

University Hall, joined to the two original University buildings. The cornerstone for it was laid a few hours after Angell's inauguration in 1871. It was the first University building for which funds were directly appropriated by the legislature. Completed in the fall of 1873, it housed administrative offices, classrooms, chapel, and auditorium. This view, taken about 1877, shows the original dome, replaced in 1896-97.

Students relaxing deep in the spring crop of grass and dandelions on the State Street side of the campus early in Angell's presidency. No one worried about manicured lawns until the modern lawnmower made its appearance.

In the auditorium of University Hall, which seated 3000 people, were held concerts, dramatic performances, graduation ceremonies, and all large events until Hill Auditorium was completed in 1913. William Jennings Bryan, Grover Cleveland, Ralph Waldo Emerson, Henry Ward Beecher, and Mark Twain were among the lecturers and artists who appeared in the old auditorium.

Completed in 1889, this building was one of the first anatomical laboratories in the country. Work in anatomy was transferred from it to the new West Medical Building in 1903.

Campus walks were muddy in winter during most of the nineteenth century. This view of the remodeling of University Hall in the winter of 1896-97 shows narrow, wooden planks providing precarious protection against mud and water.

Victor Clarence Vaughan was a member of the Michigan teaching staff even before graduation from the Medical School in 1878. In 1887 he became professor of hygiene and director of the Hygiene Laboratory, forerunner of the School of Public Health, and in 1891 dean of the Medical College.

The West Medical Building, occupied in 1903, and (at the left) the Surgical Ward.

[38]

The Amphitheater in the Surgical Ward where surgical demonstrations were held. By 1890 the medical course had been lengthened to four years, and five hundred students were enrolled in 1900.

The Catherine Street Hospitals, erected between 1891 and 1909, provided additional quarters for the rapidly growing Medical School and its services.

The Library Building, occupied in 1883 and costing $100,000, was designed to house the art treasures of the University as well as its books. When construction of the new Library was authorized in 1915 on the same site, the old fireproof book stacks were retained and still form a part of the Library stack area.

Charles Horton Cooley, at the left, sits with his back to Andrew Ten Brook, retired University librarian, in the old University Library. Cooley, son of Thomas M. Cooley and a great social theorist, was the central figure in sociology at Michigan until well into the twentieth century. John Fairlie, a distinguished political scientist, may be the man at the right.

Until the University Library Building was completed in 1883, the Library was housed in the Law Building. This view of the reading room was taken about 1877.

Jonathan Taft, first dean of Michigan's Dental College, had helped organize the American Dental Association in 1859. He pioneered in dental education and by 1903, the year of his death, the College of Dental Surgery was one of the finest in the United States.

One of the original professor's houses—standing where Clements Library now is—was fitted up in 1879 for the College of Dental Surgery (later named the School of Dentistry).

[42]

The Dental class of 1893 at work in the clinic.

The Dental College occupied makeshift quarters in old houses and abandoned hospitals for nearly twenty-five years. In 1908 it moved into the Dental Building on North University, constructed to meet its classroom and clinical needs. More than two hundred alumni attended the sixty clinics held to commemorate the event.

The staircases of the central hall of the old Museum after it had been converted to offices and classrooms as the Romance Language Building.

The old Museum, designed by William LeBarron Jenney, Chicago architect who also designed the world's first skyscraper, was completed in 1881. Situated south of Old University Hall on State Street, it housed the natural history and anthropological collections of the University until 1928. Despite its distinguished architect the building was never adequate for its purposes. Exhibit space was limited and badly lighted and the too-heavy roof had to be replaced.

Professor Jacob Reighard (?) supervising the arranging and cataloging of items in the Museum about the turn of the century.

The little "Scientific Blacksmith Shop," was the first building constructed for the exclusive use of engineering on campus. Engineering classes were held in South Hall well into the 1880's, but the 24x36-foot Laboratory Building at the southeast corner of the campus, housing a forge, foundry, shop, and engineroom on the ground floor and pattern and machine shop upstairs was completed in 1882 at a cost of $2500 for building and equipment. Students and University workmen performed most of the labor.

Surveyors from the Engineering class of 1875 pose on campus with their instruments.

The Engineering Laboratory, begun in 1885, replaced the original little shop demolished in 1887. The new building was a brick structure containing offices, classrooms, and drawing rooms as well as testing machines, steam engines, and a water tank in the tower for hydraulic work. Much of the equipment in the various labs came as gifts from tool and machine manufacturers. The tree-lined Diag is to the left.

West Engineering Building, with its Denison Arch through which the Diag passes, was completed in 1904. Its naval tank was the first such installation in an educational institution. This picture dates from the 1930's.

Mortimer E. Cooley, shown early in the century in his study on Hill Street, was appointed professor of mechanical engineering in 1881. He was dean of the College of Engineering from 1904 to 1928.

Summer surveying camps were held at various Michigan lakes late in the nineteenth century. This is the 1896 camp. At the right is Professor J. B. Davis.

Students working in the Chemistry Lab in 1887.

Moses Gomberg in the old Chemical Laboratory Building in 1890. Internationally recognized, he was professor of chemistry from 1904 to 1936 and served as assistant and instructor in the department as early as 1888, when he was still an undergraduate.

In the 1890's a wooden fence still surrounded the campus, adding its bit to a romantic winter scene.

Waterman Gymnasium, at the right, replaced earlier gymnasium facilities in 1894. Most of the funds came from private sources, including a $20,000 gift from Joshua W. Waterman of Detroit. The balcony provided a running track and the basement had locker rooms and showers. An addition to the building was completed in 1916. Barbour Gymnasium is at the left.

Barbour Gymnasium was the center of women's activities on the campus for thirty years. Quarters for social events were completed in 1896, and the gymnasium was opened in 1897. Calisthenics may have been the mainstay, but the social rooms, swimming pool, and smoky stove on which gallons of fudge were cooked, were in constant use.

Eliza Mosher, one of the first women to graduate from the Medical School, returned to the campus in 1895 as Michigan's first dean of women. Left to their own devices for more than twenty-five years, the girls were not always enthusiastic about her many innovations, such as a vigorous program of compulsory calisthenics. But in the end her warm-hearted concern won over most of them.

Old Haven Hall was the home of the Law School for sixty years. The original building, completed in 1863, also contained the University Chapel (until 1873) and the library (until 1883). In 1893 a large addition, including an imposing tower (shown here) was added on the North University side. Five years later another addition replaced the tower with a more functional new wing containing offices and lecture rooms. The building survived in this form until the fire of 1950.

Professor John Jacob Abel at work in the Pharmacology Lab in the early 1890's. He founded the first teaching department in pharmacology in the country.

Pharmacy students in the early 1890's on the steps of the Chemical Laboratory.

James Burrill Angell at his office desk in 1897 after a quarter century in Ann Arbor. He still took care of his correspondence in longhand and made do without a secretary.

Mrs. Angell entertained Ann Arbor's female Browning Society on the side porch.

President Angell in his last years headed a formidable academic clan. In this family group photographed on the steps of the President's House are his son-in-law Andrew McLaughlin, University of Chicago authority on constitutional law (back row, third from left), James Rowland Angell (second from left), who was president of Yale for many years, and Robert Cooley Angell (front steps left), who was to become a professor of sociology at Michigan.

Burke Aaron Hinsdale, educated at Western Reserve and Hiram College where he was later president, joined the faculty at Michigan in 1888 as professor of the science and art of teaching.

Silas H. Douglas, professor of chemistry and director of the Chemical Laboratory from 1846 to 1877, was one of the protagonists in the celebrated Rose-Douglas controversy of the late 1870's.

John Dewey was brought to Michigan as an instructor in 1884 by George Sylvester Morris, who had been Dewey's teacher at Johns Hopkins. Dewey was head of the Philosophy Department from 1889 until he left Ann Arbor in 1894.

Raymond C. Davis, librarian of the University from 1877 to 1905, was a New Englander who came to Michigan for his university training. Under his leadership Michigan developed by the 1890's the strongest library in the country west of Cornell.

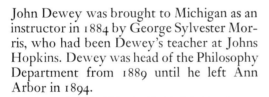

Isaac Newton Demmon ('68) headed the English Department for thirty-nine years (1881-1920). Before becoming assistant professor of rhetoric and history in 1876 he had served as principal of Ann Arbor High School.

Henry Carter Adams alternated semesters teaching political economy at Michigan and Cornell from 1880 to 1887, after which he remained at Michigan until his death in 1921. He was distinguished both for his contributions to scholarship and to government.

Faculty members took their time about marrying at the turn of the century. Fellowship, food, and rooms were provided the bachelors by the faculty's Apostles Club (supposedly named by Mrs. Angell). In 1901 members watch a chess game on the front porch (from the left): Walter B. Escott, Alexander Ziwet, Alfred H. White, Walter B. Pillsbury, John A. Fairlie, George Hulett, John Tatlock, Eugene Sullivan, Max Winkler, Mr. Carrington, Isaac N. Demmon, and Frederick Dunlap.

Dr. Angell: "I seldom stop for weather."

President Angell died in 1916 at the age of eighty-eight. Beloved by the University community and the entire citizenry of Ann Arbor and the state, his funeral procession was an occasion of general mourning.

IV

The Expanding University
(1909-29)

On April 3, 1916, President-Emeritus Angell's funeral cortege wended its way down State Street from the house on South University which had sheltered Michigan's grand old man for over half his life. The last vestiges of the nineteenth-century University were buried with him.

Seven years earlier Woodrow Wilson and Charles Evans Hughes had been among those considered by the Regents as Angell's successor, but, instead, Angell's friend and colleague, Harry Burns Hutchins, acting president 1909-10 and dean of the University's Law School since 1895, had been chosen. Hutchins, like his predecessor, was a native of New England and had received his precollegiate education there, but he was also one of the University's own sons, graduating from Michigan in 1871 at the Commencement at which Angell had given his inaugural address. Except for seven years at Cornell, Hutchins remained on the Ann Arbor campus.

Not a radical innovator, Hutchins worked toward modest change, aware of the need to correct the weaknesses of the later Angell years and interested in seeing the University move forward, but devoid of impulses to break with a past with which he had been so closely allied. Nonetheless, most of the new directions which characterized the University until World War II are traceable to Hutchins' administration.

The most dramatic feature of the Hutchins era was the rapid physical expansion of the campus. Between 1909 and 1920, the University acquired title to 114 separate parcels of land by purchase, gift, or condemnation. No longer could the original forty-acre square contain the varied activities of the University. Among the additions were the Arboretum, the Botanical Gardens off Packard Street, the site of the power plant and Palmer Field to the north of the original campus, and the land on which Prettyman's boarding house stood—where students had been well fed since 1895. The University also acquired title to the land later occupied by the Museums Building. Even the muddy hollow known to generations of students as the Cat Hole gave way to progress and became the site of the University Laundry. Many new buildings appeared on the central campus: the Natural Science Building, the new General Library, and the Chemistry Building among them.

Financing this rapid expansion of physical plant meant finding funds to supplement the University's income from the mill tax. During the last decade of Angell's presidency the University had not asked the legislature for any special appropriations, but with Hutchins the University was to become the most expensive single activity of the state. He had remarkable success with the legislature, and he needed it, for he was the first Michigan president who was constantly dependent on Lansing to carry out his programs.

But Hutchins did not confine his search for increased financial resources to the legislature. He saw the growing numbers and affluence of the alumni as a source of concrete support. The alumni loved Angell. Hutchins organized and utilized them. He spoke widely to alumni groups in Michigan and from coast to coast, urging their support and explaining the needs of the University. The results were impressive. In his ten years as president, the University received 130 private gifts totalling over $3,600,000, among them Hill Auditorium, three women's dormitories, and the Barbour scholarships for Oriental women, as well as the Michigan Union. He also obtained the promise of the Law Quadrangle.

Administratively, the casual, easygoing ways of the nineteenth century no longer sufficed. The University needed an administrative structure that could cope with increasingly complex problems. The rate of plant expansion alone required enormous outlays of manpower and skill. Hutchins did not meet this problem head on, and the burgeoning administrative bureaucracy of the twentieth century was not his creation. He made a few small changes, such as bringing a dictating machine into the president's office, but the gap really was filled by the Regents. Beginning in the later Angell years, they handled many of the details of the University's business affairs and participated actively and creatively in its building program. It was a regental Golden Age, and the ability of these men clearly matched their power and influence. Arthur Hill, Levi Barbour, William L. Clements, Benjamin Hanchett, Lucius L. Hubbard, Walter H. Sawyer, Chase Osborn, Junius Beal, Frank Fletcher, and James O. Murfin were men whom the state could clearly claim as among its most distinguished leaders. The Regents gave freely of their material wealth, as generous gifts such as Hill Auditorium and Clements Library attest, but they also provided daily administrative, legal, and business guidance to the University. They filled a need, and they filled it well for almost a generation.

In the Hutchins era also began the twentieth-century University's concern for student welfare. The University took increasing responsibility for housing its students. For the first time since the Tappan years dormitories, at first only for women, appeared on the campus—Helen Newberry, Betsy Barbour, and Martha Cook residence halls. The real beginnings of a Student Health Service date from 1913, when undergraduate agitation hastened the opening of an ambulatory service for student patients. The proper protection of student health also motivated official attention to campus sanitation and the examination of Ann Arbor's water supply.

The second half of Hutchin's term was greatly disrupted by World War I. First, conflicts, real and imagined, arose over faculty allegiance to and sympathy with the protagonists; later, when the United States entered the war, most of the male students were enrolled in the Students Army Training Corps, with an unfortunate lack of cooperation between the demands of military training and those of academic programs. The results were frequently chaotic, and demoralization was completed by the disastrous influenza epidemic of 1918. But by the end of 1919 the campus was free of temporary barracks, most of the uniforms had disappeared, and while inflation posed a threat to the living standards of the faculty, the signs of war had largely disappeared. Nearly 13,000 of the University's sons had served the country in some capacity or another, and over three hundred had lost their lives.

Meanwhile, Hutchins' second five-year term was drawing to a close and at seventy-three he was ready to retire. The Regents again looked for a successor. On July 1, 1920, Marion LeRoy Burton took office as president of the University of Michigan. Iowa-born, educated at Carleton and Yale, Burton came to Ann Arbor from the presidency of the University of Minnesota. He had a genius for getting on with people and a remarkable talent for organization. These qualities, combined with his force and drive, resulted in impressive accomplishments during his relatively brief tenure as president.

Burton set out to revitalize the University. He reworked its administrative structure, setting up formal channels for its governance and the handling of its business not unlike, at least in principle, what we find today. He increased the level of state support of the University by obtaining a substantial increase in the millage rate from the legislature, but more significantly through substantial special appropriations for new buildings. Faculty salaries were raised. New divisions and new schools were established. The Department of Geography dates from this era. The School of Education received an independent status in 1921 and the School of Business Administration, developed from courses in the Department of Economics, in 1924. Training in Social Work entered the curriculum for the first time in these years. Concern for student welfare continued and expanded, and a Housing Bureau was established. In 1921 the Office of Dean of Students was authorized by the Regents, and intercollegiate athletics and physical education were formally organized as two departments.

During the Burton years University activities moved into the larger world. Plans were made for establishing the University's Lamont-Hussey astronomical Observatory in South Africa. William Hobbs led University expeditions to study mountain formations in the western United States, Hawaii, and Japan. Michigan-sponsored anthropological expeditions under Carl Guthe studied and collected in the Philippines. The Near East archeological expeditions led by Francis W. Kelsey and others permitted the University to assemble its great collection of papyri.

But the most substantial contribution of Marion Burton himself was the leadership and direction he gave to the University's building program. For the first time the University systematically shaped a comprehensive scheme, based on a general campus plan, for an expanding physical plant designed to meet its present and future needs. The response to requests for building money to succeeding sessions of the legislature was on the whole sympathetic. The long list of buildings completed largely during the Burton administration includes: University Hospital, Yost Field House, Angell Hall, the Law Quadrangle, the East Medical Building, University High School, Couzens Hall, and the East Engineering Building. Burton's contribution to the University's physical plant is visible on the campus today.

The dynamic energy which characterized Burton as a man and a leader may have undermined his health. Most of his last year in office was marked by serious illness. At first his ultimate recovery was hoped for, but the strain had been too great, and he died of heart failure February 19, 1925. The University community could well mourn his loss.

By September 1925 the Regents had decided on Clarence Cook Little as Burton's successor. Little was only thirty-six when he was elected president of the University of Michigan. He had made a reputation as a research biologist and had embarked on an administrative career as president of the University of Maine. Outspoken and progressive in his educational and social views and impatient to see them effectuated, Little found himself on a campus which was still mourning his predecessor and which deeply revered its own traditions of nearly a century. Vigor and leadership were always appreciated at Michigan but radical change had always been suspect.

In many ways Little foresaw the great issues that were to preoccupy the large universities later in the twentieth century. He felt that the needs of students were being generally lost sight of in the University system as it had developed by 1925. Believing strongly in the wisdom of a basic education which all University-trained people would share and which would provide them with a community of discourse regardless of what profession they chose, he saw this could be accomplished in a University College with its own faculty attended for two years by all students. He considered the modern university to be neglectful of the individual student's welfare, and he sought creative solutions to the problems of increasing size. Freshman week was one of his innovations. He believed strongly in the dormitory system and in special programs and curricula designed to meet the needs of women.

His programs could not be implemented without controversy. His plan for a two-year general studies program aroused opposition in the professional schools which saw their training unduly lengthened. The Literary College faculty also was opposed. Little alienated Ann Arbor rooming house operators with his plans for a greatly expanded dormitory system. Outside the Ann Arbor community his support of radical social ideas such as birth control and euthanasia collected a formidable clerical and fundamentalist opposition. Students were distressed at his dicta calling for less emphasis on athletics and by the ban on student automobiles. At one time or another the *Michigan Daily* branded him with such epithets as "Tyrant," "Boss," "Reformer," and "Pussyfoot." But when Little decided to abandon the fight and resign, the *Daily* headlines mourned, "Michigan Turns Its Back on a Genius."

And possibly Michigan had—but with a sigh of relief that was clearly audible from the legislative halls of Lansing to country churches in the northern counties and even in the lecture rooms on the campus itself. Little probably gave his own sigh of relief as he retired from University administration to pursue once again the distinguished career as research biologist which had previously occupied him. Some of his programs remained, but his larger ideas for changing the Michigan campus, such as the University College plan, were abandoned at his suggestion when he submitted his resignation.

Harry Burns Hutchins ('71), Owosso superintendent of schools, Mount Clemens lawyer, assistant professor of rhetoric and history, dean of the Law School, became president of the University in 1909. He was born and raised in New England, but his Michigan connections were deep. He belonged to the University and to the state as no other president ever had.

Alumni Memorial Hall was a controversial project dubbed "D'Ooge's Palace" and "The Mausoleum" by the students, who much preferred to see alumni effort go into fund-raising for the Michigan Union Building. However, the classic structure on State Street attracted alumni support. Completed in 1910, the building relieved congestion in the Library by providing space for the University's art collections.

[64]

The academic procession emerging from University Hall in 1912 had to compete for color with the ladies' hats and parasols. This was a gala occasion celebrating the seventy-fifth anniversary of the University at Ann Arbor. The ceremonies themselves were held in a huge tent pitched alongside Waterman Gym.

Huron Street, looking east from Main Street toward the campus about 1912, was brick-paved but still a thoroughfare for horse-drawn vehicles.

The Regents dined with President Hutchins at his home in December 1910. Standing, from the left, Luther L. Wright (superintendent of public instruction), Shirley W. Smith (secretary), Walter H. Sawyer. Seated, from the left, Chase S. Osborn, George P. Codd, William L. Clements, Frank B. Leland, Dr. Hutchins, President-Emeritus Angell, Junius E. Beal, Loyal E. Knappen, John H. Grant.

After Commencement (about 1912) Governor Chase S. Osborn, President Hutchins, and Dean Mortimer Cooley stroll across the campus.

Regent Levi Barbour made several generous gifts, principally to the University's women: Barbour Gymnasium, Betsy Barbour Residence, and the Barbour Scholarships for Oriental Women.

Hill Auditorium, built on the site of Professor Alexander Winchell's octagonal house on North University, was the gift of Regent Arthur Hill. Acoustical problems for an auditorium of this size were considerable but were solved almost completely.

Although the School of Music was not completely integrated into the University until 1929, the University had appointed a University organist shortly after the Frieze organ was moved to Hill Auditorium. Palmer Christian filled this post from 1923 until his death in 1953.

The Natural Science Building was completed in 1915. Albert Kahn was the architect, and the cost was less than half a million dollars, although two and a half million cubic feet of space were acquired.

The demolition of the old Library's towers.

The General Library, which stands on the site of the old Library, was dedicated in 1920.

The spacious and well-lighted reading room in the General Library. The frescoes in the lunettes above the windows at the ends of the main reading room are by Gari Melchers.

William Warner Bishop, librarian from 1915 to 1941, began his career as a classical scholar. During his tenure the General Library was constructed, the University's distinguished papyri collection was acquired, and the Library of Congress classification system was adopted.

The new Homeopathic Hospital, completed in 1900, provided for homeopathic patients until the two medical schools
were consolidated in 1922.

Wilbert B. Hinsdale was the last dean (1895-1922) of the
Homeopathic Medical School. He had the distinction of pur-
suing two successful careers. When the Homeopathic School
was discontinued in 1922 he became curator of the University
Museum's collections in Michigan archeology. His monumental *Atlas of Michigan Indians* is still a classic.

From 1909 to 1922 the controversial Homeopathic Medical
School had its own program in all branches of clinical medicine. Dr. Claudius B. Kinyon, gynecologist, about 1914, is
instructing his students at a demonstration clinic.

In the Hutchins era women's gym classes featured formal calisthenics.

Filibert Roth, fourth from the left in the first row, relaxes with his boys at the forestry camp in Saginaw Forest, May 1918. Several of the students are in army uniform. They were part of the SATC.

The coeds were joining the boys in summer classes at Biology Camp on Douglas Lake in 1915. The man is Norman Wood, curator of birds in the Museum.

The Engineering Camp on Douglas Lake in Cheboygan County was acquired in 1909. It was later renamed Davis Engineering Camp in honor of Joseph B. Davis.

These engineering students were running tests on refrigeration plants in 1913.

Jesse Siddall Reeves joined the faculty as professor of political science in 1910, marking the formal beginning of the department, although courses in the subject had been given earlier. He taught international law and served his government as well as his University with distinction.

Arthur Lyon Cross lectured to generations of students on English history in a galleried room in old Mason Hall, the north wing of University Hall.

Mortimer E. Cooley and Joseph B. Davis at the engineering camp in 1917.

[75]

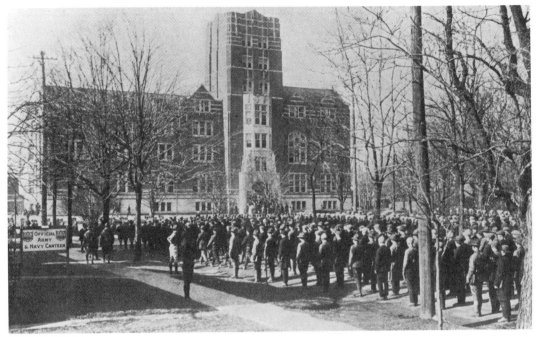

The Student Army Training Corps (SATC) drawn up before the Michigan Union in the fall of 1918. The uncompleted Union served as a barracks for 800 men and mess hall for 4000 during World War I.

University students being sworn into the U.S. Navy in Waterman Gymnasium in 1918.

Marion LeRoy Burton, red-headed, energetic, and loaded with charm, was one of the greatest and most persuasive orators of his day. As Frank Robbins wrote, "His voice was a wonderful natural instrument, always completely under his control, and his platform appearance was compelling."

Angell Hall was completed in 1924 at a cost of $1,077,000. President Burton had insisted that adequate quarters for the College of Literature, Science, and the Arts be the cornerstone of his building program. For many years the chief administrative offices of the University were on the first floor. The architect's sketch shows the additions planned for the original structure but never built: the tower to the rear and the wings at either end.

Aerial view of the campus early in 1923 showing Angell Hall under construction, Clements Library almost completed, and the site cleared for the Museums and East Medical buildings. Martha Cook dormitory appears at the extreme left, but the Law Quadrangle has not yet been begun.

The William L. Clements Library, gift of Regent Clements, replaced one of the original faculty houses. Completed in 1923 it houses a distinguished collection of rare books in American history.

The rare book room in Clements Library.

Harry Burns Hutchins and Marion LeRoy Burton on the terrace of the Michigan Union.

The East Medical Building housed the classrooms and laboratories of the basic sciences — anatomy, bacteriology, physiology, and histology—and was one of the major achievements of the Burton administration. Together with the clinical facilities of the new University Hospital it gave Michigan adequate and modern quarters for its Medical School program.

Dr. G. Carl Huber provided medical students with their basic instruction in histology and embryology until his death in 1934. During much of his forty-five years of service with the University he was also professor of anatomy, and from 1928 to 1934 he served as dean of the Graduate School.

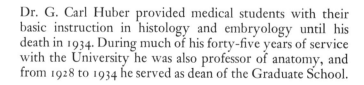

Patients were moved into the University Hospital from the old Catherine Street building in 1925. The new Hospital was long overdue, and eight years had passed since the legislature made the first appropriation for it. In fact, the uncompleted building was boarded up for several years. The Hospital provided space for more than 700 beds and cost nearly $3,500,000. More than $400,000 of this amount was spent for equipment.

President Burton hands a diploma to a pretty Michigan coed of the early 1920's. Shirley Smith, secretary of the University, chats behind the huge pile of rolled diplomas.

Junius Beal of Ann Arbor served as regent from 1908 to 1940, the longest service of any of the University's regents.

Claude Van Tyne, distinguished historian of eighteenth-century America, joined the University faculty in 1903, became chairman of the History Department in 1911, and served in that post until his death in 1930.

Robert Frost lived in Ann Arbor from 1921 to 1923 as a recipient of a fellowship in creative art. Burton had proposed the fellowship as a stimulus to creativity in the academic community. Chase S. Osborn, former regent, and an anonymous donor supplied the stipend. Frost was also brought back for the year 1924-25.

Enoch Peterson (at the left) and Francis W. Kelsey (second from the right) with archeologists at the site of the University's excavations at Carthage in 1925.

Alfred H. Lloyd joined the faculty of the Philosophy Department in 1891. He was dean of the Graduate School from 1915 until his death in 1927. Upon the death of President Burton he served as acting president until President Little was appointed.

William Herbert Hobbs led the University's geological and meteorological expeditions to Greenland in the 1920's. Hobbs (center) and colleagues huddle in an arctic sailing craft.

The East Engineering Building was completed in 1923 to house the departments of Chemical and Metallurgical Engineering, Aeronautical Engineering, and Engineering Research. By 1920 the College of Engineering was enrolling more than 2000 students.

A new physics building (now named the Harrison M. Randall Laboratory of Physics) was another of Burton's acquisitions. Ready for use in 1924, it provided the Physics Department with adequate laboratories for the first time.

Clarence Cook Little, handsome, brilliant, and tactless, served a stormy term as president of the University from 1925 to 1929.

Commencement in 1926 was held at Ferry Field. The women are just turning off State Street to enter the gate.

Henry Ford received an honorary degree at the 1926 commencement.

The Law Quadrangle, gift of William W. Cook ('80, '82*l*) was begun in 1923 and completed a decade later. The largest single gift ever received by the University, these buildings, consciously reminiscent of the colleges of Oxford and Cambridge and the Inns of Court in London, are the most luxurious on campus. Even in the early 1920's they cost $16.35 per cubic foot. Clements Library at a cost of $9.82 was the closest contemporary runner up.

The Law Library main reading room.

Left: In the Law Quad.

Below: Ralph William Aigler ('07*l*) joined the Law School faculty in 1908, training many generations of lawyers before his retirement in 1954. From 1913 to 1955 he also served on the Board in Control of Intercollegiate Athletics.

The University's Lamont-Hussey Observatory at Bloemfontein, South Africa, realized a life-long dream of W. H. Hussey. The building housed the large refractor.

Right: William J. Hussey, professor of astronomy and director of the Observatory from 1905 until his death in 1926, and Richard A. Rossiter, who was long to be in charge of the University's Lamont-Hussey Observatory at Bloemfontein, on their way to Africa as the Lamont Astronomical Expedition. Hussey died in London shortly afterward.

Below: The Museums of Anthropology, Zoology, and Paleontology are housed in the University Museums Building completed in 1928. This photograph was taken about 1930 before Carleton Angell's puma-like creatures were set in place to guard the front entrance.

V

The University in a World of Change (1929-51)

ALEXANDER GRANT RUTHVEN became president of the University of Michigan on October 5, 1929. Ruthven was not a Michigan undergraduate alumnus. He received his baccalaureate from Morningside College in his native Iowa, but did his graduate work and spent the rest of his professional career at Michigan. As a teaching fellow he had searched late at night for appropriate specimens for the freshman zoology labs in President Angell's garden. He was a distinguished herpetologist who had led many expeditions in the field. However, his administrative talents as director of the University Museums inevitably called attention to other ways in which he might serve the University. President Little had drafted him (despite Ruthven's reluctance) for the position of dean of Administration, a job today equivalent to a bevy of vice-presidencies.

Ruthven's administration coincided with a series of external crises which began with the great Depression of the 1930's and included the onset of the Korean War. Certainly, no previous president's tenure had encompassed a commensurate impact of outside events on the affairs of the University. In spite of this the arresting characteristics of the Ruthven years, if viewed as part of the internal history of the University, while modified, were not completely controlled by what was happening in the larger society.

Ruthven's greatest innovations were administrative. No matter what the times, he would have had an impact in this area. As a zoologist Ruthven looked for orderly relationships and schematic sense. He was also aware that

[*90*]

no president could any longer personally or intelligently watch over the varied activities of so complex a body as the twentieth-century state university. And he distrusted the academic feudal baronies which had eroded centralized direction as personal control by the president became impossible. Ruthven inaugurated what was essentially a cabinet system. Vice-presidents with overall responsibility for broad divisions of the University's affairs originate with his administration. Executive committees for departments, colleges, schools, and independent agencies take their place on the academic scene. Previously, deans and department chairmen had been free to appeal directly to the Regents when they saw fit. The days of this kind of autarchy were over, although the autocratic control of a powerful dean or chairman over his own faculty was not so easily eliminated. Many a college or departmental executive committee was to prove little more than a futile gesture for at least another quarter of a century.

There were other characteristics of the early Ruthven years. Research was officially encouraged and given meaningful financial support for the first time. No longer was it treated as the well-meaning stepdaughter of a heavy teaching schedule. In part this resulted from the Rackham funds being available to the faculty, but more importantly from having at the helm a man who understood the symbiotic relationship between research and teaching.

As in other administrations, some new buildings were financed by public funds. In 1930 the University Elementary School was completed from appropriations made directly to the University by the state. There were similar additions to the University Hospital. As in previous decades gifts continued to provide significant additions to the University's plant. The Law Quadrangle, Burton Tower, the Baird Carillon, and the Rackham Building were the direct gifts of generous donors. However, for the first time, if one ignores the early land grants, federal funds played a major role in financing the building program. Without them there would have been little construction in the late 1930's.

Changes also occurred in the academic structure. In 1929 Ann Arbor's excellent proprietary School of Music merged with the University. In 1931 Architecture and Design became a separate college, completely independent of Engineering. Psychology split formally from the Department of Philosophy in 1929 upon the death of Robert M. Wenley. The School of Public Health was established as a separate unit in 1941. The institute, separate from college or department (but also indirectly related to both), was born. The Institute of Public Administration, the duties of which originally included the supervision of social work, began the procession, followed by the Institute for Human Adjustment, the Neuropsychiatric Institute, the Institute of Archaeological Research, the Institute for Fisheries Research, and the English Language Institute. For the first time the University also became conscious of the need for making special provision for preserving its own history. The extensive archives of the University were collected and cared for by a new manuscript library, the Michigan Historical Collections.

Meanwhile, the world, the nation, and the University were experiencing the traumas of the great Depression. Banks closed, investments and savings vanished overnight, and many a wage earner of factory or office found himself without a job. At first the University's enrollments decreased, but this reaction was short-lived as federal programs provided the wherewithal for young people to continue in school. Faculty salaries were reduced and staff positions eliminated, but not all the Depression's effects were negative. The FERA (Federal Emergency Relief Administration) and NYA (National Youth Administration), by providing funds for projects which employed student help, gave significant assistance to many a faculty research idea. Federal funds helped to build the Michigan dormitory system. West Quad, East Quad, Victor Vaughan for medical students, Stockwell Hall, and the Interns Residence at the Hospital had substantial subsidization from the WPA. The Health Service Building also received a federal grant.

The most significant and far-reaching result of the Depression, however, was the University's permanent loss of tax support independent of legislative appropriation. The mill tax was an inevitable casualty of the times. Real property could no longer be expected to furnish the major share of the tax base on the state as well as on the local level. The property tax for state purposes was repealed and with it the University's millage share. The state of Michigan sales tax solved many of the immediate fiscal problems, but meant the end of the century-old financial independence of the University. The University retained its constitutional status as an independent branch of the commonwealth, but dependence on the legislature was inevitable, balanced somewhat since World War II by the increasing role played by the federal government in supplying funds.

By Commencement in 1937, when the University celebrated its centennial under the state constitutions, the Depression was waning and the next world holocaust was still two years away. The new Baird Carillon in the Burton Tower chimed the hours, the impressive new building housing the Horace H. Rackham School of Graduate Studies was a campus showcase, and, more important, the Rackham research funds were giving the faculty resources seldom available elsewhere in the country, for supporting an individual faculty member with a significant research idea.

But progress and increasing prosperity soon gave way to the demands of World War II. Foreign students found themselves both without funds and physically unable to return home. Young men enlisted or were drafted. Many of the faculty commuted to Washington or joined the armed forces. Still others devoted themselves to war-related research in their Ann Arbor laboratories. There was little of the internal conflict on campus which had accompanied World War I. President Ruthven provoked a short-lived flurry of protest when he addressed the students just after Pearl Harbor suggesting that their elders, not they, were to blame for the state of the world and that their proper place was in school continuing their studies until called elsewhere. But even enemy aliens and Japanese-Americans were accepted with intelligent sympathy and no trace of hysteria.

Ruthven struggled with success to retain the essential integrity of the University. He refused to let it be completely absorbed and controlled by the armed services, although he made its facilities available to them. Once again the campus filled with uniforms. Army Specialized Training Programs (ASTP), Navy programs, the Judge Advocate General's School, and the Military Intelligence Language School absorbed many of the resources a rapidly dwindling population of male undergraduates left unused. In time, a growing trickle of veterans, invalided out of the services, returned.

Victory in Europe and the Far East brought a new set of problems. The enrollment mushroomed with veterans returning in a flood—the postwar peak being 21,363 in 1948. The married student with a deserving wife and a child or two appeared on campus in significant numbers for the first time. It was impossible to house everyone. Temporary accommodations at the makeshift village built for war workers at the Willow Run bomber plant provided minimal quarters to which students could, at best, adjust. University Terrace Apartments, completed in 1947, were the first postwar permanent construction on campus, but provided for only a fraction of the need. The faculty was overworked and classes were too large, but there was compensation in the excitement of teaching a new variety of student body. Young men eager to telescope time, achieve a meaningful education, and return to or acquire the career they had temporarily abandoned stimulated the harried teachers. Many of these veterans eventually swelled the ranks of the Graduate School. In all, the University provided training for 32,745 returned veterans of World War II.

The campus was expanding as fast as limited construction facilities permitted, but not fast enough to ease the congestion. The Administration Building, the first major addition to the central campus area, was rapidly followed by the new School of Business Administration. A substantial addition to East Quad and the completion of Alice Lloyd Residence in 1949 helped alleviate the dormitory crush. The hospital complex received its first major addition since before the war when Women's Hospital was finished in 1950.

Research mushroomed as rapidly as space could be found. The need for proper laboratories may have kept the physical sciences confined to more orthodox quarters, although they too proliferated in temporary buildings at Willow Run airport, acquired by the University in 1947, but the social sciences were content with anything available—from old houses to abandoned hospitals. The Survey Research Center joined the University in 1946. The Center for Japanese Studies was organized in 1947. A year later the Research Center for Group Dynamics came to Michigan. This development of interdisciplinary centers for service, instruction, and research outside the traditional departments was but the beginning of what was to become a veritable flood of similar agencies.

In 1951, with most of the problems of postwar readjustment under control, Alexander Grant Ruthven retired as president of the University. He considered himself an alumnus president, and his nostalgic affection for Michigan, which had granted him his Ph.D., was great. He also saw himself as head of a university which in some measure was still manageable as an academic family. In an institution which had an enrollment of many thousands he welcomed personal contact with students, made himself available to those brash enough or desperate enough to seek his advice or help, and frequently, even if there was a fortuitous quality to these contacts, played a direct and paternal role in the lives of individual undergraduates. He found it more congenial to act as headmaster to students and as academic leader and coordinator to the faculty than to perform as fund raiser, entrepreneur, or "image."

He very personally charted the University's course through two decades of great stress for the institution itself, the nation, and the world. He successfully recruited and used the help of a body of professional administrators (eventually even professional fund raisers) as the times demanded, but he also preserved the essence of a more intimate era, a personal touch whenever accident or circumstance made it possible. Only James B. Angell had served longer as Michigan's president. The worlds in which these two men lived and worked were far apart, but both cherished not only their achievements as leaders of a great University, but also their contributions to the development and education of the young men and women entrusted to their care. Angell was no doubt a real person to a far larger proportion of undergraduates than Ruthven, but Ruthven assiduously nourished and cherished what contact and influence he had with a student body so gargantuan that most presidents would have dealt with it only in general terms. Somehow he found a real point of personal contact with a Michigan student body that had grown to the size of a small city.

Alexander Grant Ruthven, a member of the faculty since 1906, followed Clarence Little as president in 1929. He had received his doctorate degree at the University. Little had chosen Ruthven as dean of administration, a post which prepared him for the presidency, but Ruthven's many faculty friends and local ties also helped him to allay the storms of the Little years.

This aerial view of the campus area in 1930-31 shows part of the Law Quadrangle still under construction. Burton Tower and the Rackham Building were yet unbuilt.

The President's House at twilight during the Ruthven years. The old side porch where the Angells took the air had long since gone. The new presidential study can be seen to the rear at right.

Generations of students stood under the Maynard Street trees and listened to the music coming from the practice rooms of the old School of Music Building. Erected when the School was in-dependent of the University, it continued to be used until about 1960.

The construction of Burton Tower in the depths of the depression was financed by contributions from alumni and friends, and even gifts in kind—gravel, cement, hardware—were accepted from local merchants and builders. Cash contributions ranged in amount from $2.00 to $5000.

The University Elementary School, attached to University High School, was completed in 1930.

Nursery school children through sixth graders provided a laboratory for the School of Education programs.

Architecture finally moved into a home of its own in 1928. This view shows its gardens with the columns and other fragments of architecture just after World War II.

Joseph R. Hayden returned from naval service in 1918 to an assistant professorship in political science. He was a specialist on the Philippine Islands and was chosen by Frank Murphy as his vice-governor of the Islands from 1933 to 1935. In 1937 he became chairman of his department, a post he held until his death in 1945.

Emil Lorch came to Michigan as professor of architecture in 1906. He had worked with Sullivan in Chicago and had taken an advanced degree at Harvard. In 1931 when the department became the College of Architecture and Design and was separated from the College of Engineering, Lorch *(right)* became its first director.

John L. Brumm began his University career in the Department of Rhetoric, from which the Journalism Department originated. When it was made a separate department in 1929, Brumm became its first chairman, a post he held until his retirement.

Above: The Apostles (faculty bachelor's club) still held forth in the 1930's. Here they are gathered once more on their front porch. They played an annual baseball game with ex-members who had become the "henpecked husbands."

Left: Dr. Reuben Kahn, distinguished director of Pathology Laboratories and professor of clinical bacteriology and serology, working in his laboratory in 1938.

The Rackham Building, the gift of Horace H. Rackham and his wife Mary, was completed in 1937. It provides quarters for the Graduate School offices and study halls, recreation lounges, exhibition rooms, and lecture halls. Thirty buildings, many of them student rooming houses, had to be removed to clear its two-block site.

The Health Service Building, which replaced inadequate quarters in the old Homeopathic Hospital, was completed in 1940. Almost half of the cost was paid by WPA funds. Most of the University's share was raised by issuing Health Service bonds.

Alice Lloyd served as dean of women from 1930 until her death in 1950. She belonged to a distinguished University family. Her father was Alfred H. Lloyd, dean of the Graduate School and acting president when Burton died.

Alumnus Frank Murphy, attorney general of the United States (a former governor of Michigan and later a justice of the Supreme Court), and Dr. Ruthven at the dinner in October 1939 celebrating Ruthven's tenth anniversary as president of the University.

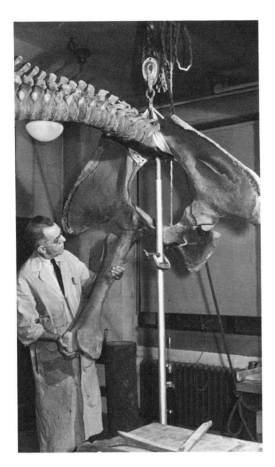

A dinosaur skeleton being assembled for exhibit in the Museums Building by Preparator W. H. Buettner.

Harley H. Bartlett in the Botanical Gardens, of which he was director from 1919 to 1955. He joined the faculty in 1915 and was chairman of the Botany Department from 1923 until 1947.

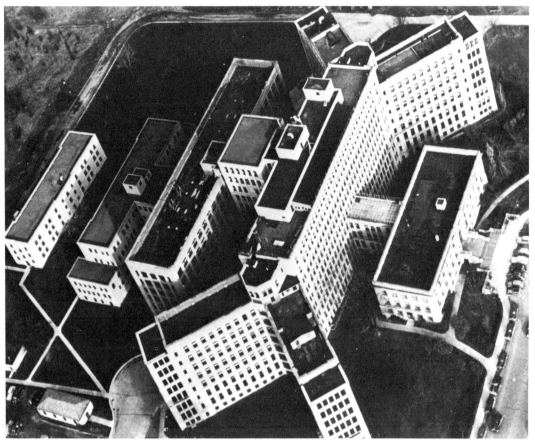

An aerial view of University Hospital about 1940. The Internes Residence, extreme left, was completed in 1939. The entrance to the Hospital was remodeled after World War II.

The National Music Camp at Interlochen affiliated with the University Summer Session in 1941 and offered degree credit courses by University faculty members.

Maneuvers were held in the Arboretum early in 1942 as the University's ROTC units prepared for an active role in World War II.

Naval units march to Ferry Field.

Ann Arbor streets resounded to the clatter of marching men in the early 1940's. The JAG's in battle dress parade up Main Street to aid a war bond drive.

Naval units in dress whites parading on Ferry Field.

Training Japanese language experts was one of Michigan's World War II contributions. This was the second class (May 1943), in front of Angell Hall.

The Judge Advocate General's School personnel
in the garden of the Law Quadrangle.

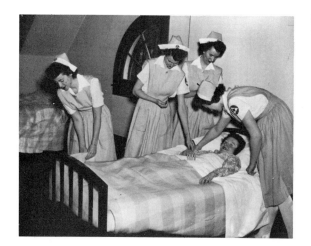

Coeds trained as nurses' aides during the war years.

Many of the men in JAG School were older lawyers. This fifth class (October 1942) is at work in Hutchins Hall.

Co. B-4 lining up for chow in front of the Union.

Coeds dancing with soldiers in the Grand Rapids Room of the Michigan League. The women were willing hostesses at the local USO.

Singing around the piano at the recreation center in Harris Hall.

The School of Public Health Building, a gift of the W. K. Kellogg and Rockefeller Foundations, was built during World War II. Contributions to the wartime search for quinine substitutes and influenza vaccines were made here. Health officers to serve in occupied countries at the end of the war were also trained.

The Administration Building was completed in 1948, the first new permanent structure to grace the central campus area since World War II. It cost $2,500,000 and necessitated closing access to State Street from Jefferson Street.

President Ruthven with the Regents in November 1949 in the new Administration Building. From the left: K. Stevens, R. Bonistell, O. Eckert, R. Hayward, Dr. Ruthven, J. Herbert, A. Connable, Vera Baits, and Dr. C. Kennedy.

English Language Institute (ELI) mushroomed after the war. Professors Charles Fries, Robert Lado, and Rafael Junquera using a recording device in 1949. By 1964 more than 11,000 students from eighty-four countries had taken advantage of the Institute's services.

The Institute for Human Adjustment's Division of Gerontology pioneered in studying the problems of aging in the postwar period. This group of senior citizens discussed community living at a conference held in 1949.

The School of Business Administration was the first "skyscraper" classroom building in the campus area. It was built at a cost of more than $2,500,000.

The cornerstone for the School of Business Administration was laid in May 1947, and the building was completed in 1949.

Carl Milles' fountain, a memorial to Thomas McIntyre Cooley, plays on the mall between the Michigan League and Hill Auditorium.

Michigan's program in naval architecture and marine engineering dates from 1881-82, when Mortimer E. Cooley offered the first courses. Students in 1950 are loading a model of one of the last big Mackinac ferries for testing.

The Center for Japanese Studies was the first of several interdisciplinary area study programs developed after World War II. A field study center was established in Okayama, Japan.

The Survey Research Center is best known for its studies of voting behavior in national elections, but teams of researchers work on many problems.

After World War I the Observatory was no longer adequate for modern astronomical work and a rural site free from atmospheric pollution was essential. The new lenses, completed in 1950, were installed in the tower built on University lands at Peach Mountain near Portage Lake.

Old Haven Hall, originally the Law Building, succumbed to a dramatic fire in June 1950. Much went up in smoke, including most of the books and pamphlets in the Public Administration Library.

The fire in old Haven Hall necessitated rapid completion of Haven and Mason Halls, which replaced old University Hall. They were dedicated in 1952. The lobby, soon dubbed the "fish bowl," looks out on the Diag.

The Ruthvens with undergraduates at the last student tea held in their home before the president's retirement.

VI

At Mid-Century
(1951-67)

BY THE SPRING OF 1951 a curious University community was speculating as to Dr. Ruthven's successor. Despite his long tenure no break in continuity this time could possibly match the shock of Angell's retirement in 1909. Then it had seemed almost unbelievable that anybody else could be president of the University of Michigan. Now the campus was far too full of new faces —staff and faculty, as well as students—to create a pervasive "end of an era" atmosphere. There had been no change in leadership for over two decades, during which more than 76,000 degrees had been granted to the University's students, and the world had changed mightily. But year by year at an increasing rate the University was changing too, for change was the ethos of the times.

On May 21, 1951, Harlan Henthorne Hatcher accepted the presidency of the University and took office September 1. Handsome, articulate, urbane, with an attractive and photogenic young family, Hatcher was easily forgiven his Ohio State antecedents by even the most ardent football fan.

His administration was to face its own series of crises, keyed more to the state of Michigan politics and the burgeoning American birthrate than to universals of world depression, war, and precarious peace. Problems were as diverse as obtaining adequate appropriations from an almost bankrupt state government with a legislature unwilling to initiate necessary tax reform, retaining and recruiting a distinguished faculty in the face of nationwide academic competition never matched before, dealing with the inevitable alienation of students as undergraduate education was both challenged and eroded by the demands of growing professional and graduate programs and proliferating research obligations, and, not least, encountering the repercussions of the stress and strain imposed on America and her citizens by living in a world peopled in part by enemies who not only challenged her military power but also her basic ideological commitments. The University survived—not without trauma and not without conflict—with the inevitable combination of retreats, advances, and compromises.

When Hatcher arrived the University was experiencing a welcome pause in the enrollment explosion. For a brief year or two the declining birthrate of the 1930's was reflected in a drop in admissions which permitted the administration to marshal resources. In 1952 less than 17,000 students registered at Ann Arbor in contrast to the 1948 postwar peak of more than 23,000. But in 1953 the totals again began to mount, and the enrollment became a vital issue by the end of the decade. In 1960 the Regents formally decided that growth should be controlled and adopted a flexible formula limiting enrollment in each school or college to the number of students who could be accommodated without impairment of educational standards. Despite its ambiguity this was courageous action at a time when competition for state appropriations among the several tax-supported institutions of higher learning was particularly keen, and when some were freely admitting all applicants.

The University under Hatcher's leadership continued to accept as one of its major functions the responsibility for providing undergraduate education, and the plan for a new undergraduate residential college with its own faculty was one solution devised to keep the quality of undergraduate education high. A four-year Literary College honors program was also tailored to the needs of the superior student. However, there was no denying the University's increasingly rapid drift toward becoming a center for advanced study. By 1959, 38 percent of its students were in the Graduate School or in graduate professional programs beyond the baccalaureate degree. By 1965 the number had risen to 42 percent.

In addition to more orthodox methods of expanding its facilities, the University switched to a radical new calendar in 1964-65. Three full semesters were fitted into a single twelve-month year. June graduates became a thing of the past. Commencement now preceded Ann Arbor's May flowers, spring vacation shrank to a long weekend in early March, and the influx of new freshmen for the fall term enlivened the sultry days of late August. Total enrollment figures raced past the thirty-thousand mark and made the post-war bulge seem mild by comparison.

The appropriations crisis reached its peak in 1958-59 when the legislature's support of the University was actually reduced at a time of cutthroat national competition for faculty and rapidly increasing enrollments. In the early 1950's faculty salaries had finally reached their prewar level as adjusted for cost of living, but meanwhile per capita income in the United States had made spectacular gains. Other universities and colleges were beginning to bring academic compensation into line. Michigan could not. In the five years after Sputnik, faculty salaries at the University of Michigan fell from third to seventeenth place among the nation's colleges and universities. Fortunately, the crisis was short-lived and the erosion of faculty quality was relatively slight. But the University had been unable to expand its physical plant adequately or increase the size of its staff in preparation for the spectacular enrollment growth of the early 1960's.

While legislative appropriations went down and then slowly began to climb again, money from sponsored research contracts was increasing rapidly. Scientific programs benefitted most. In 1961-62 the University had more contracts with the National Aeronautics and Space Administration than any other university in the country. In the mid-twentieth century sponsored research was the instrument through which the federal Treasury became a major source of University income for the first time since federal land grants were made to the Catholepistemiad early in the nineteenth century. Funds from business, private foundations, and endowments were dwarfed in comparison. Unsponsored research undoubtedly suffered. The Rackham funds which had seemed so munificent in the 1930's were relatively tiny by the 1960's. A Rackham grant could still provide meaningful research support in the humanities, but it was completely inadequate for major work in the sciences.

Although expansion of the University's physical plant may have been delayed by the state financial crisis, never has total building exceeded its pace in the 1950's and 1960's. There are now campuses instead of a campus. In the spring of 1952 the first earth was turned on the University's new tract on the north side of the Huron River. North Campus was designed as a home for such bedfellows as the applied engineering sciences, the new residential college, and programs in the performing arts. The Mortimer E. Cooley Building, the first structure completed there, was followed by other engineering research buildings, crowned by the tower of the Institute of Science and Technology Building. Library stacks, the printing plant, the new School of Music Building, a student center, and acres of apartments for married students also sprouted on these rolling hills.

The controversial Flint Branch, generously supported by Charles S. Mott Foundation funds, was the University's first attempt to furnish undergraduate education spatially removed from the Ann Arbor campus. The University of Michigan possessed a "branch" for the first time since the 1840's, but this time the branch was designed not as a preparatory school but as an equivalent undergraduate facility. In October 1961 the Dearborn Center, designed to provide degree programs in the arts and education as well as work study programs in business and engineering, was dedicated.

On the main campus, sprawling far beyond the boundaries of the original forty acres, the most spectacular expansion occurred on the hillsides surrounding University Hospital. The Outpatient Clinic, the Kresge Research Institute, the Medical Center Library and medical classroom buildings, the new School of Nursing, the Institute for Mental Health Research, a children's psychiatric center, and a new children's hospital fanned out around University Hospital, which still provided basic inpatient care. Medical School enrollments expanded rapidly in the 1950's to make maximum use of these new facilities.

Contingent to both the Medical Center and earlier dormitories, Mary Markley Residence, the biggest housing unit of them all, spread along Washington Heights. On the original campus the Undergraduate Library was fitted into a spare corner, and old University Hall was razed to make way for the new Mason and Haven Halls. On East University the Physics-Astronomy Building provided another impressive skyscraper. Beyond Forest the new Women's Pool lay alongside Palmer Field. On the west side of State Street, South Quad, the Student Activities Building, and the Institute for Social Research sprouted in city blocks where student rooming houses had

recently stood. And scattered strategically about were the parking structures, for in mid-twentieth century cars were almost as important in the University's building schemes as classrooms, offices, and laboratories.

This physical explosion of the University was matched by a constantly expanding range of its concerns. Interdisciplinary centers multiplied.
Much of the research budget of the University was concentrated in the sciences, but creative ideas and effort supported by modest funds covered a
much wider spectrum: the quest for peace—the Center for Research on Conflict Resolution; careers for women—the Center for Continuing Education
for Women; better undergraduate programs—The Center for Research on
Learning and Teaching. This is a small sampling of the interests explored by
the new centers.

The major conflict, but not the major crisis, of the Hatcher administration reflected American uneasiness at facing the fact that there were
enemies as well as friends in our world of precarious and interrupted peace.
A congressional subcommittee, looking for enemies within (perhaps as a
more available scapegoat), chose to investigate the political beliefs of three
University faculty members. The repercussions rivaled the nineteenth century's Rose-Douglas case in emotional intensity, but the wounds healed
more quickly, perhaps because the University community was now so large
that a far smaller proportion of its members felt involved. Also over the years
orderly processes for handling conflict between administration and faculty
had become institutionalized, and spontaneous appeals to townspeople, to
colleagues, and to regents were much less likely than in an earlier era.

The other area of conflict during the Hatcher years was with students. This did not develop fully until the 1960's, and even then the student
rebellion against the "multiversity" and general student alienation from
society were so intertwined that the issues were muddy. Michigan's troubles
did not reach the proportions experienced elsewhere, but there could be no
doubt that students were restless. The University was very big, and it would
not get smaller. Never again would the undergraduate loom as large in its
total concerns as in the prewar era. It was equally impossible for the faculty
to find the communality that had unified an earlier teaching body.

In 1963 the state of Michigan adopted a new constitution which
technically preserved the Regents' constitutional status as a body independent

of both legislative and gubernatorial control, but which nonetheless ambiguously charged another board with overall responsibility for higher education in the state. The uncertainties thus generated pointed up the temptation to feel nostalgia for presumably simpler days—for earlier anniversaries when it was easier to catalogue achievements and feel confident of continuing progress toward goals that were both possible and universally accepted. Perhaps the uncertainties were as great in 1912 or 1937 or 1941 as in 1967. Problems are solved and then forgotten in the intervening ongoing action. Michigan ended her first century and a half still in a position of national leadership in the academic community, and in some ways, more important, her basic central position in the educational plan of the state of Michigan—as conceived in 1817 or 1837—is essentially intact.

Harlan Henthorne Hatcher, native of Ohio and trained at Ohio State University, became Michigan's ninth president on September 1, 1951.

[*133*]

The Diag view in the early 1950's was not much changed from that of an earlier era.

The air force sent officers here as students in 1952 to study guided missiles. The guidance system for the BOMARC missile was developed at Michigan.

The Atomic Energy Commission (AEC) sponsored research with the bubble chamber.

Above: The Frieze Building, the remodeled old Ann Arbor High School and Public Library with a new addition made possible by closing Thayer Street between Washington and Huron, housed speech, modern languages, and social work in the Hatcher era.

Right: Albert E. White, first director of the Department of Engineering Research, turned the first spade of earth for the Cooley Building on North Campus in the spring of 1952. Vice-President Wilbur K. Pierpont looked on.

The announcement of the validation of the Salk polio vaccine was made in Rackham Auditorium in April 1955 by Dr. Thomas Francis, Jr. From the left: Dr. Hatcher, Dr. Francis, Dr. Salk, and Basil O'Connor.

Even on the crowded campus of the second half of the twentieth century the Law Quadrangle
retained its quiet charm.

The Flint branch of the University opened in 1956. It was devoted exclusively to upper division undergraduate education, and for its first ten years only senior college courses were taught.

Students using the Language Lab at the Flint branch.

Lillian Hellman with students at a Hopwood Room coffee hour. Many Hopwood award-winning manuscripts have been published. The portrait of Roy W. Cowden, long-time director of the Hopwood awards, hangs on the wall.

President Hatcher and Regent Eugene Power explaining to legislators the urgency of the University's needs during the financial crisis in 1956.

English, Journalism, and some language and social science departments held many of their classes in Mason Hall in the late 1950's.

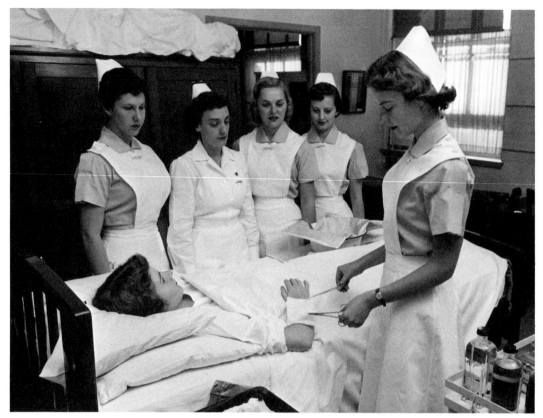

The four-year degree program had replaced the earlier three- and five-year nursing programs in 1954. Nurses waited another four years until 1958 before their crowded quarters were replaced by a new building.

Professor Kasimir Fajans at his last chemistry class before retirement in May 1956.

The cyclotron being housed in its own building on North Campus.

The Undergraduate Library, air-conditioned and with all its books available on open shelves, was the favorite place for study in the 1960's, but burgeoning enrollments soon overtaxed its facilities.

In 1957 Regent Frederick C. Matthaei gave the University land on which to relocate the Botanical Gardens. The new buildings, designed by Alden Dow, were dedicated in June 1962. Michigan could now boast the third largest herbarium in the Western Hemisphere.

One of the new parking structures ringing the campus. This one is on Catherine Street.

In a speech made on October 14, 1960, at two o'clock in the morning, John Fitzgerald Kennedy first launched the idea of a Peace Corps from the steps of the Michigan Union.

[148]

A new $17,000,000 dental center was begun in 1966. The crowded clinic in the old Dentistry Building had limited space and made adoption of a year-round calendar impossible.

At times in the mid-1960's the outer boundaries of the campus resembled a gravel pit and the center of town looked like a bombed city. New construction both by the University and by private developers was the culprit.

The University's Computing Center was a busy place in the 1960's, analyzing data from the hundreds of research projects. Seated at the left is Robert Bartels, the director of the Center.

Eiro Saarinen designed the plan for the North Campus development. The tower in the center is the Institute of Science and Technology Building completed in 1963.

This aerial view of North Campus was made in 1965. The Music School is center front, the site for the new dormitories is at the left, below the Northwood Apartments for married students. The North Campus Commons is in the center.

The Physics-Astronomy Building provided needed space for the basic sciences when it was finished in 1963. In the five years after Sputnik enrollments in undergraduate science courses almost tripled.

By the mid-1960's the walks were a solid mass of bodies and vehicles when classes were changing. The "fish bowl" between Haven and Mason Halls is in the background, and behind that is the back of Angell Hall.

[*154*]

Edward R. Murrow made the Commencement address in the Stadium in 1961.

Michigan's astronaut alumni, James A. McDivitt and Edward H. White II, with Governor Romney, received honorary degrees at a special convocation in June 1965.

[*155*]

The new School of Music on North Campus faces an artificial lake. Designed by Eiro Saarinen, the building was dedicated in the fall of 1964. The School of Music finally had the accommodations first promised in the mid-1930's.

The new Dearborn Center was dedicated in 1961. The campus was a gift of the Ford Motor Company, which also supplied generous funds toward the construction of a new building.

The Institute for Social Research Building was dedicated in 1966, the first new building devoted entirely to research in the social sciences.

The Medical Center in the mid-1960's. The Kresge Research Building and Library flank the old Hospital to the west. The Outpatient Clinic and Women's Hospital are on the east. The new Charles Mott Children's Hospital is to replace the parking lot near the Outpatient Building.

Lyndon Baines Johnson with Harlan Hatcher and Erich Walter. President Johnson was Commencement speaker in May 1964 and used the occasion to make his first formal statement on the Great Society.

VII

Student Life

Bed and Board

ALL STUDENTS WERE HOUSED in North Hall and South Hall from the opening of the University in 1841 until President Tappan decided in 1856 that students were better off uncloistered and should live in town. Originally, a tutorial system in the British tradition was planned, but only once was a tutor actually in residence. The men were grouped in three-room suites—a study with a closet to hold the wood supply and two adjacent bedrooms. Classrooms were on the first floor. A woodpile was behind the buildings, and students were supposed to do their log-splitting out-of-doors. Of course, the uncut wood was moved in where it was warmer, and the result was creative mutilation of the study floors. The dormitories had no arrangements for feeding students, but board could be obtained at several houses adjacent to the campus for one dollar to two and a half dollars a week.

Theoretically, Tappan abolished the dormitory system because he felt that students would lead a more normal life in town. His convictions became more urgent when a tripling of the Literary Department enrollment in four years strained the meager classroom facilities. With the abolition of dormitories the era of the rooming house began. Fraternities, which provided the only alternative housing for men for over three-quarters of a century, always served only a minority of University students.

Food and lodging might be obtained under the same roof or a man might room in one house and board elsewhere. Students' letters home were full of complaints about the quality of food. The students did a good deal of moving from place to place in search of better accommodations, and occasionally made arrangements to prepare their own meals. A barrel of apples or a side of salt pork from home was always a welcome addition to the diet. Given the long Ann Arbor winter, few rooms were warm enough before central heating to pose much of a threat of spoilage.

By the time women arrived on campus in the 1870's the boarding-house and rooming-house pattern was well established. No one worried about providing the young women with special quarters, they simply fitted into the system as best they could, with Mrs. Angell keeping a motherly and vigilant eye on them. Actually, Mrs. Angell's concern grew as the campus population of females increased. To begin with, intellectual girls were something of an oddity. The faculty wives saw them as not quite proper, and it took a couple of decades before they became desirable brides. John Dewey married a Michigan coed, and Alice Freeman Palmer, one of the ablest of Michigan's early female graduates, found herself an academic husband as early as 1887, but Eliza Mosher, Lucy Salmon, and other pioneering graduates saw their destiny as competing and excelling in the world of men. They did well at it.

The rooming-house era at Michigan lasted well into the twentieth century. For the most part students lived in rooming houses and ate in boarding establishments. Boarding clubs were run by enterprising students working their way through school, but more often boarding-house proprietors were Ann Arbor entrepreneurs furthering one of the city's major industries —providing services for students.

Supervision of housing for women dates from 1904, when the first "league house" was opened as a result of agitation for protection by the newly organized Women's League. League houses rented only to women, parlor privileges (for the entertainment of callers) were provided, and quarters were inspected by the dean of women or her staff. Concern for adequate housing for women soon spread. Newberry and Martha Cook dormitories were constructed in 1915, Betsy Barbour in 1920. Several smaller residences were also acquired by the University. The first large dormitory for women, Couzens Hall, was designed exclusively for University Hospital student and graduate nurses. No large dormitory for general use was built until Mosher-Jordan was completed in 1931, and then only after a controversy with rooming-house operators who feared the University would put them out of business. Although the number of privately owned league houses fell from seventy-six to twelve in the years immediately following Mosher-Jordan's completion, overcrowding was soon a problem again and Madelon Stockwell was finished without objection in 1940.

Residence halls for men were erected in the late 1930's. The major opposition to them came from the fraternities, who at first saw them as a deliberately devised instrument for the ultimate destruction of the fraternity system. Originally, there were high hopes for a house system modeled after English colleges, and some vestiges of this plan still remain in the older quadrangles, but by the time South Quad was constructed after World War II, costs were such that it could not be carried out. Dormitory living for men never assumed the proportions that it did for women, and no new dormitories for their exclusive use have been built since 1951. Instead, parts of the men's residence halls have been made coeducational, as have parts of Mary Markley House.

Construction of Alice Lloyd Hall and Mary Markley House temporarily eased the overcrowding in women's residences after the war, and league houses survived and flourished. However, by 1961 these supervised girl's rooming houses had dwindled to a mere dozen, most of which operated as sorority annexes.

Meanwhile, the married student had arrived on campus. From 1945-50 he tended to be a veteran, older than the normal undergraduate and willing to accept all kinds of inconveniences to further his education. The lucky ones were housed in modern fireproof apartments in University Terrace adjacent to the Arboretum. A few found privately owned quarters. The rest lived in relatively primitive conditions at Willow Village or in the trailer court behind the Coliseum. Willow Village was at least a challenge. The units were heated by coal stoves, and the only hot water was provided by the boiler on the wood-burning or coal-burning cook stove. The campus was ten miles away by bus. But a nursery school and recreation center helped provide a sense of community.

The married student was not a postwar phenomenon—he remained.

In the 1960's a quarter of the students were married. Those who were single wanted living arrangements similar to those of their married peers. By mid-century the trend was again consciously individualistic. The privately rented apartment was the norm for men and upperclass women. Coeds trotted across the Diag carrying their grocery bags. The local supermarkets were crowded on Friday afternoons with male "apartment teams" doing the week's marketing. Skyscrapers ringed the campus and furnished undergraduates a new kind of free-wheeling "superquad." Quarters were not necessarily more luxurious or less crowded, but they were presumably private—private at least from the eyes of administrators and their surrogates. The student wanted to be on his own. Another rigor—that of the real estate agent with his leases, high rents, and high-speed elevators—began to be felt. Student apartment dwellers asked for a benevolent University's protection once more in their dealings with the private entrepreneur whose services they had so ardently welcomed. The circle had come full again.

David Mack Cooper attended the University 1844 to 1848. He says an extravagant classmate spent more than $500 a year. This sounds like rank exaggeration to impress his father with his frugality. Cooper expected to spend another $21 (in addition to the amount itemized), bringing his total expenditures for the semester to $40.

ATTENTION!
INDIGNATION MEETING

The Citizens of Ann Arbor, are requested to meet at the Court House this evening, at 6 o'clock, to take into consideration the conduct of the *FACULTY* of the University of Michigan, in *Expelling* all the Students belonging to Secret Societies!

December 10, 1849.   MANY CITIZENS.

Left: Fraternities experienced opposition early, at first from the faculty. They did not provide housing for their members until 1875.

Below: In 1856 Stephen Northrup began a letter on his fancy "M" stationery by boasting to his friend about the availability of girls in his new rooming house. Rooming houses replaced the dormitories that fall. On the next page he writes: "Jackson and I are rooming together, board ourselves and are digging in to study our best." Students were doing their own cooking more than a hundred years ago.

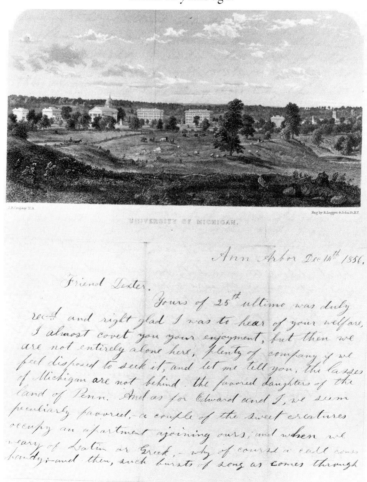

Student room in the 1890's. Tea kettle and chafing dish testify that culinary skills on the part of the male are not a recent development.

Girls' rooms in the gay nineties were complete with cushions, potted palms, and pretty little tea sets.

H. Caldwell Smith and W. K. Bromley shared this room in the tower of the Delta Kappa Epsilon house at the turn of the century. Not all students lived in such relative opulence.

J. H. Port's attic room at 636 South Thayer (where the Law Quad now is) is much more Spartan.

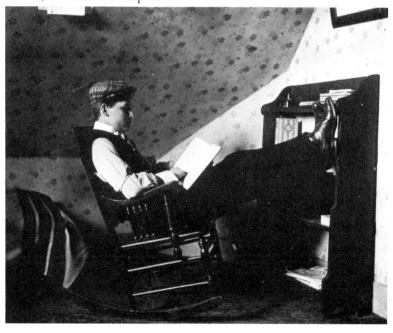

Helen Newberry Residence, completed in 1915, provided the first dormitory housing for students since President Tappan moved the boys out of North and South Halls in 1856. Newberry, the gift of the Truman Newberry family, originally housed seventy-nine coeds. Betsy Barbour House, at the left, the gift of Regent Levi Barbour, was completed in 1920.

The sun room at Betsy Barbour was furnished in the latest mode—cretonne and wicker.

Martha Cook Building, the first of William W. Cook's generous gifts
to the University, was completed in 1915, a few months after Newberry. The street was still unpaved, but the appointments within were
luxurious.

The Blue Room in Martha Cook Building. (The Red Room was a
reproduction of a room in a sixteenth-century manor house.)

By 1942 Palmer Field was ringed with women's dormitories—Couzens (not shown), to the north, was the first, then Mosher-Jordan, and Stockwell (at the right).

Alice Lloyd Hall, opened in the fall of 1949, was the first residence for women completed after World War II.

Sports and Games

The muddy northeast corner of the campus square, where an informal game of cricket could be played, was the sum total of Michigan's athletic plant for the first fifteen years after the University opened its doors in Ann Arbor. In 1856 a manual exercises shed was built in the same neighborhood, and two years later it was fitted up as a primitive gymnasium with a few poles, cross-bars, and rings. It was unheated, however, and of little use during the worst winter weather.

Cricket was the first organized sport. By 1860 a regular team set up wickets right on State Street. Three years later a baseball diamond was also laid out in the northeast campus corner, which had become the area for physical activity and where Waterman Gym still stands. By 1867 the baseball players had uniforms and were competing for the state championship, defeating the Ann Arbor team 30-26. The team also played Detroit and Jackson.

Of course, these groups had no official standing and no one worried about eligibility. However, in 1873 interested students formally organized the Football Association and three years later the Baseball Association; in 1878 these merged to become the Athletic Association with the avowed aim of raising funds to build a gymnasium.

This student-controlled Athletic Association raised about $6000 in twenty years, but it was obvious that the students would never reach their goal by their own efforts, and when Joshua Waterman's gift of $20,000 in 1891 turned the gymnasium into a reality they contributed their kitty to the newly formed Board in Control of Athletics—a part of the University proper, which has governed Michigan's athletics ever since.

By this time intercollegiate sports had begun, though they were conducted on a rather casual basis. In 1878 Michigan played its first intercollegiate football game with Racine, and in 1881 the team journeyed east and managed to lose to Harvard, Yale, and Princeton. Ten years later a coach was acquired, a Yale graduate who was earning a Michigan law degree. He lasted only one year, but was replaced by another Yale graduate. This time the team made a foray into the West and the schedule for 1892 sounds very familiar—Wisconsin, Minnesota, Northwestern, and Chicago. Coaches continued to be men attending the University's professional schools until the turn of the century.

In 1896 the Western Conference was formed, and in 1901 Fielding Harris Yost came to Ann Arbor as coach. The modern era in Michigan athletics had begun. From the beginning the Conference squabbled over eligibility and subsidization of athletes, with Michigan in favor of more liberal rules. Michigan parted company with the Conference in 1908, but rejoined it again in 1917. The most burning issues were the propriety of the training tables, lures for high-school athletes, and the matter of only three years' eligibility.

Meanwhile, Yost had fashioned the Champions of the West, and his point-a-minute teams of the early twentieth century became one of the national wonders. He concluded his very first season by taking his undefeated boys to Pasadena to participate in the first Tournament of Roses game, where they won over Stanford, 49-0. Such athletic prowess pointed up the need for better physical facilities, and in 1902 Dexter Ferry gave the University the seventeen acres at Hoover Avenue and State Street which became Ferry Field and where most of the buildings comprising Michigan's athletic plant still stand. Ferry Field was also outgrown, and in 1927 the new stadium was dedicated.

Baseball was part of the intercollegiate athletic program from the beginning, and tennis matches were held as early as 1897. But basketball did not become a varsity game until 1917, although an abortive effort to organize a team was made in 1909. In 1921 swimming, wrestling, and hockey were added, and six years later golf. Competition in gymnastics dates from 1931.

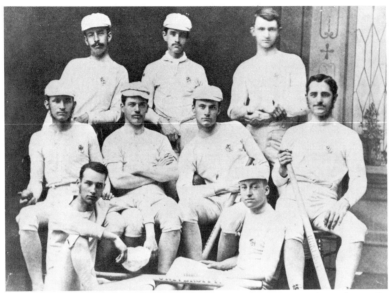

Baseball and cricket competed for popularity in the 1860's and 1870's. This is the baseball team of 1875.

This football team defeated Racine 7-2, May 30, 1878, at White Stocking Park, Chicago. It was Michigan's first intercollegiate match. Irving K. Pond, later a University architect, is on the left in the middle row.

The ladies' crew, with Miss Cora Bennison as stroke, must have been organized soon after women were admitted to the University. These coeds skulling on the Huron were all members of the Classes of 1878 or 1879.

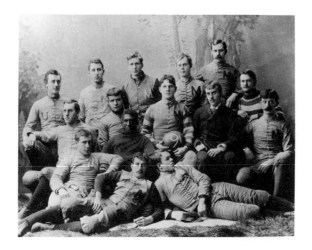

Although the numerals on the ball would seem to indicate this is the team of 1891, it is actually the team of 1890. Fourteen handsome stalwart men, but hardly enough for unlimited substitution.

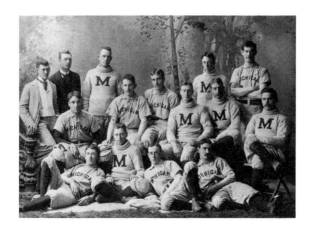

The baseball team went east in 1890 and met Cornell and Colgate.

The engineers were the intramural champions in 1894. The man holding the ball also played on the varsity.

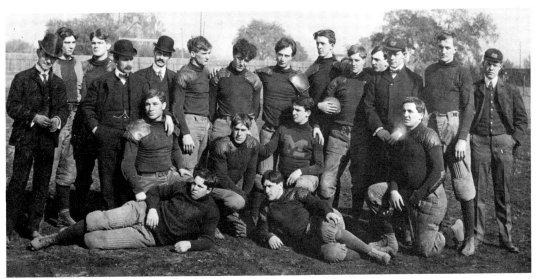

Michigan's first Tournament of Roses' team at Pasadena's Tournament Park in late December 1901, preparing for the New Year's Day victory over Stanford. Coached by Yost, the team included the well-remembered Hugh White, Neil Snow, Boss Weeks, Dan McGugin, and Willie Heston.

Both Chicago and Michigan were members of the Western Conference in 1903 when Nelson Kellogg came in first in the two-mile race at the track meet.

Fielding H. Yost, who had been a member of the University of West Virginia football team, came to coach Michigan football in 1901. His tenure was as impressive as his "point a minute" teams. He was head football coach until 1926.

Palmer Field was surrounded by woods rather than dormitories in 1910. This match was for the women's frosh-soph championship.

Women's fencing teams in Barbour Gym about 1915.

Michigan fans at the Michigan Central Depot, seeing the football team off for the Harvard-Michigan game of 1914.

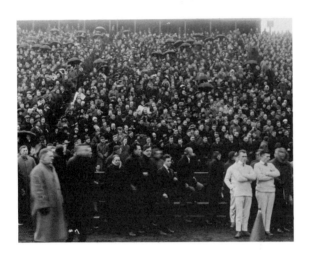

The University of Michigan trounced Michigan Agricultural College (later to become Michigan State University), October 12, 1916, while the fans at Ferry Field tried to keep off the rain.

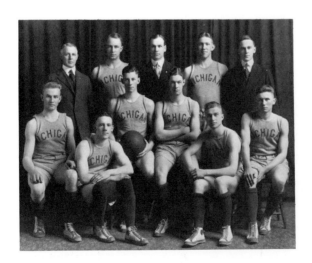

The varsity basketball team of 1918 was coached by Elmer D. Mitchell, later chairman of the Department of Physical Education for men.

[*180*]

Yost Field House was dedicated in 1923. It was large enough to accommodate a full-sized football gridiron, basketball floor, or track meet. However, its space for less than 8000 spectators at a basketball game was outgrown when basketball became more and more popular.

Michigan's badly needed new stadium was ready in 1927, the year after Yost completed his coaching career. Originally, it seated 87,000 and the stands were at ground level on the west side.

The Intramural Sports Building completed in 1928 on Hoover Avenue provided the average male student with facilities for intramural sports and games.

Fritz Crisler instructs his backfield during the 1939 season. The players, from the left, are Forest Evashevski, Bob Westfall, Tom Harmon, and Fred Trosko.

Benny Oosterbaan took his champions to the 1951 Rose Bowl by air. Lowell Perry stands behind Oosterbaan. Ted Kress and Fred Baer are in the front row, and Dick Beison and Ted Topor stand next to the coach.

Coach Matt Mann with the freshman relay team of 1946. He produced many championship swimming teams during his long tenure, 1924-54.

Lowell Perry on a long run against Minnesota, October 1952.

Timberlake set for a play during the 1963 season.

Cazzie Russell, No. 33, shoots during the Minnesota game in the 1965-66 season.

Organizations

Student life at Michigan in the mid-nineteenth century revolved around the Classes. It was the Classes which competed with and harassed each other, and many a chapel session ended with the juniors rushing the seniors on the North Hall stairs. The Classes held exercises and exhibitions, banquets and frolics, organized and impromptu. Everyone knew everyone else, and an identity in the University community was easily established.

Clubs also flourished from the very beginning, organized by the undergraduates to perform more specific functions. Literary societies were formed in the late 1840's, and there may have been a glee club as early as 1848. By midcentury fraternities, debating clubs, musical organizations, athletic teams, the Student Lecture Association, and the Students' Christian Association were all flourishing. Clubs, societies, and class activities continued to be important throughout the nineteenth century. There was no formal supervision of these activities by the University, and discipline was handled by the president and the faculty when the need arose.

The coeds were the first to look for an overall organizational structure. After all they had special needs. Excluded from most of the campus activities by their male colleagues and with wretched housing conditions, they founded the Women's League in 1890 in the hope of solving some of their problems. The League was University-wide from the beginning, including women in medicine, law, and other departments as well as undergraduates in the Literary College. Within a year it began raising money for a social center for women. It organized systematic orientation and induction of new women students on the campus, and it worked hard and fruitfully to improve women's housing. Social parlors were part of the new Barbour Gym, and the women set up the system of league houses by which they could live; they also began to adopt rules and regulations for their governance—enforced by themselves—which were the first seeds of student self-government. Nearly all the women in the University attended League teas and banquets, as did many of the faculty wives as well.

Meanwhile, the rapidly growing number of male students was taxing the informal arrangements of an earlier era. University supervision of student activities dates from 1902 when a series of scandals, including misuse of Student Lecture Association funds, caught the University Senate's attention, and the forerunner of its Committee on Student Affairs was established to provide overall supervision. The men had no club house or coordinating agency to act as a focus for their extracurricular life. To fill this lack, representatives of the leading campus organizations initiated the Union movement in 1903. Fund-raising campaigns for the Union Club House began almost immediately. County fairs, minstrel shows, and alumni dinners helped to swell the coffers, and the Union was able to purchase the Thomas M. Cooley house on State Street and open it for use in November 1907.

The Michigan Union soon outgrew these quarters. Additions were made to the rear, but a new building was essential. This involved a monumental money-raising effort in which alumni and undergraduates cooperated. The new building was begun in 1916 and was still unfinished when World War I halted construction. A loan was obtained to complete it to a point where it could be used to billet soldiers being trained on campus, and it was finally finished in 1919.

With the new Union Building attracting widespread Union membership and the Women's League boasting that almost every girl on campus had paid its dues, voluntary membership and dues in these university-wide organizations were discontinued in 1919. All students became members, and dues were part of the student's fees.

The League and the Union became the vehicles through which student government developed. Class elections were held under Union auspices. The Student Council was its creation. Unofficial and nonvoting student participation in disciplinary matters was channeled through the judiciary committees, and in 1947 representatives of the Women's and Men's Judiciaries were made voting members of the official all-University disciplinary body.

When the women obviously outgrew their quarters in Barbour Gym they raised money for an ambitious new building. In the spring of 1929 the Michigan League was opened, but because of the Depression that began that fall the planned endowment fund did not materialize and the building had to be self-supporting. In 1965 the Women's League ceased to exist as a separate organization. Women and men were united in the Activities Center.

The literary societies, Phi Phi Alpha (1842), Alpha Nu (1843), and Literary Adelphi (1857), followed by others like them, furnished an outlet for creative activities in a period when the curriculum was rigid and electives were few. The University provided space—even in its first building—for the meetings. Papers and orations were presented in rooms in North Hall.

Right: Many of the early critical literary efforts of students were in the form of broadsides. This 1857 broadside lampoons President Tappan and the faculty.

Below: Physics was executed each year after an elaborate trial, when the course was completed. The tradition began in the 1860's and lasted into the twentieth century.

Les San Souci (which also called itself the University Band), in 1859, was one of several early musical groups organized by students. Frederick Arn (extreme left) was killed three years later at the Battle of Shiloh in the Civil War.

Glee Club members in 1870 wore tasseled class caps and treated a Jackson audience to a program of college songs. This was their concert debut, and a hundred fellow students journeyed with them on a special train.

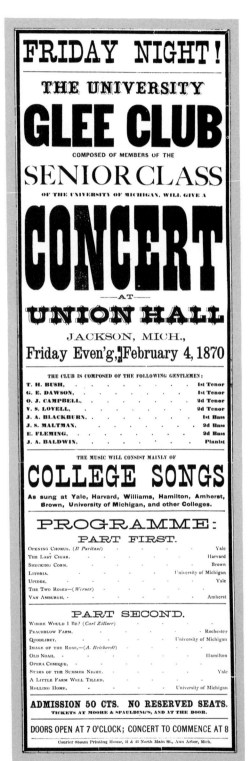

The Glee Club program given at Jackson in 1870.

The "Smokers of '76"

The editors for 1878 of *The Chronicle*, a bi-weekly and later weekly journal (1867-91). The paper was frankly antagonistic toward faculty and Regents most of the time.

Left: The first J Hop was held in 1872. These 1891 belles probably danced at Hangsterfer's Hall on the corner of Main and Washington streets.

Below: After graduation came the reunions. The Class of 1874 gathered at Commencement time twenty-five years later.

The Glee Club made a successful tour of the West in 1896. Here the members are at the summit of the Marshall Pass.

The University Band by the turn of the century was really a band. It had played at football games as early as 1897.

The Michigan Daily was called *The Michigan Daily News* from 1901 to 1903. This was the last completely independent student newspaper produced at Michigan. The next fall the Board in Control was established. Early *Daily* editors made considerable sums from their "private enterprise." The editors are in the city room, about 1902.

OYEZ! **OYEZ!** OYEZ!

AFTER THE BATTLE

All ye haughty, supercilious vagaries of imbecile minds; all ye eidolous of insolence and effrontery; all ye flamboyant, bombastic bugaboos; all ye abject, sordid grovelling pests; all ye gaudy pretentious swabs; all ye livid yellow yaps; all ye egregious asses;

HIST!

to the defiance of the efficacious Freshmen; the modest, retiring, unobtrusive, yet the all powerful, virile and domineering entities that sway the acres.

HEED!!

the edict of the seasoned men who are preparing to dole out death and dire destruction to all second-year, secondary, second-class, second-rate opposition (at the time appointed) on

Black Friday, Oct. 9, 1908

at 8 bells in the eventide, we the all conquering, will meet you of the priggish demeanor neath the Freshman Oak

THERE

mid the crunch and roar of the imbroglio, mid the cries of despair and anguish, mid the heart-rending sobs of "Oh! Woeful Day," and "Have Mercy! Percy!" mid the hoarse, exultant shouts of the victors, and the soft stridulations of the dead underfoot, while the air is viscid with lamentations, we will hack and haggle the heads from your bodies, and, mounting these vacuum environments upon staves, will place them in conspicuous places throughout the campus acres.

Phenozygous and cryptozygous; dolicocephalic and acrocephalic; flat-heads and round-heads; pig-heads and sap-heads; block-heads and cone-shaped heads; all will be severed alike, to draw the gaze of the morbid, to rot and moulder; and to stand, an indubitable, irrefrangible, incontrovertible proof of the superiority of

Fresh over Soph

Signed, Michigan, 1912.

"Rushes" on one class by another, often announced by broadsides, were common almost from the beginning of the University. Hazing and general mayhem were the order of the day.

The rivalry between the Laws and the Lits was at fever pitch in 1900.

The 1907 pushball contest at Ferry Field.

Left: The Michigan Union Opera grew out of the Minstrel Shows put on to raise money for the Union. *Michigenda,* the first opera, was staged at the Athens (Whitney) Theater in the spring of 1908.

Below: The Comedy Club was organized in 1896 and produced plays on campus until 1935, usually during J Hop weekend. *Pomander Walk* was performed in the Whitney Theater in 1915.

Right: The coeds in 1910 had spring maypole dances.

Below: The freshmen and and sophomores taking part in the annual tug-of-war in the spring of 1914.

Colleges and departments held formal parties. The engineers and their guests in 1911.

At the J Hop in 1914. In the early years of the century the dance was held in Waterman Gym, and the students and their guests always formed a block M for their photograph albums.

The Michigan Union was the most ambitious structure of its kind in the country at the time it was built. President Hutchins presided over the ground-breaking ceremonies in June 1916. Except for the swimming pool and library the original building was completed in 1919. For many years women could not use the front entrance.

All That Glitters was produced by Mimes, the Union's dramatic society, in 1915 with the usual all-male cast.

"Rope Day" for Michigamua, senior student honor society founded in 1901. Members of the Tribe choose juniors to carry on as "true Michigan men."

Braves and bucks of Michigamua on the way to a powwow at Whitmore Lake about 1903.

The Druids by their sacred rock, about 1920. This senior honor society of the Literary College dates from 1909. Torch in hand, gowned and hooded, members march each spring to initiate the new "Awenyds."

The Sphinx, an all-campus junior honor society, was founded in 1906, in the golden decade for such societies. These neophytes rode a sacred chariot and waded in Milles' Cooley fountain looking for "the River Nile."

Mortar Board, senior women's honor society was founded in 1906. Dean Myra Jordan is in the center of the second row from the top in this group of the members in 1918.

The Junior girls presented *Gold* in 1920. Their senior guests marched in a body to the theater wearing their caps and gowns for the first time.

Right: The Mimes Theater was originally the ballroom and dining-hall addition of the old T. M. Cooley house when it served as the first student union. In 1921 the building was converted into a theater and continued as the center of dramatic activity on campus until the Lydia Mendelssohn Theater was opened in the League Building.

Below: The Michigan League cornerstone was laid in March 1928. Mrs. Arthur H. Vandenberg is addressing the crowd. President Little can be seen in the group directly to her left.

[207]

The Michigan League Building was the great alumnae project of the 1920's. Planning and fund raising began in 1921. The building was completed in the spring of 1929. The site was purchased from a legislative appropriation, but the building itself was paid for by gifts of alumnae from all over the world.

The Ruthvens at the University's International Center with girls from the Philippines at their booth at the International Fair. Foreign students began to enroll in the University early in its history, and close ties with the Far East, fostered by Dr. Angell's diplomacy, have attracted many students from Asia.

The percussion section of the concert band at Hill Auditorium, March 1948.

[*209*]

The Goodfellow edition of *The Michigan Daily* was sold on a dripping wet Diag by campus leaders in 1943 to raise money for student charities.

In March 1949 a successful *Froggy Bottom* was the first Union opera produced after World War II.

Shakespeare's *King Lear* was produced in April 1950. Play production in the Speech Department began with a single course in 1915. By the 1930's its offerings were dwarfing the strictly amateur efforts.

Michigras in the 1950's carried on the tradition of the county fairs and carnivals held as early as 1902 to raise money for a student union.

The Glee Club, directed by Philip Duey, performing in the fall of 1954. The next summer they gave sixteen European concerts.

Students voting in front of the Union at the 1950 Student Government Council elections.

The Marching Band, aided by the alumni band, forms the block M in the Michigan stadium in the 1960's.

1. Court House.
2. County Jail.
3. Fire Engine House
4. M. C. R. R. Depot.
5. A. A. & T. R. R. Depot.
6. Cemetery.

SCHOOLS.

7. Union School.
8. First Ward.
9. Second Ward.
10. Third Ward.
11. Fourth Ward.
12. Fifth Ward.
X German School.

CHURCHES.

13. Baptist.
14. Congregational.
15. Episcopal.
16. Evangelical.
17. Lutheran.
18. Methodist.
19. German Methodist.
20. Presbyterian.
21. R. Catholic.
22. Universalist.

PUB. BY J.J. STONER, MADISON, WIS.,

ANN

PANORAM

WASHTENA